THE MAFIA FILES

THE MAFIA FILES

CASE STUDIES OF THE WORLD'S MOST EVIL MOBSTERS

AL CIMINO

ARCTURUS

ARCTURUS

This edition published in 2014 by Arcturus Publishing Limited
26/27 Bickels Yard, 151–153 Bermondsey Street,
London SE1 3HA

Copyright © 2014 Arcturus Publishing Limited

ISBN: 978-1-78212-777-2
AD003676UK

Printed in China

CONTENTS

INTRODUCTION

In 1970, the Racketeer Influenced and Corrupt Organizations Act (RICO) was passed in the United States. This provided for extended criminal penalties for acts performed as part of an ongoing criminal enterprise, such as the Mafia. Significantly, it became possible to prosecute Mafia bosses who had ordered an offence, as well as those who had actually committed it.

Under RICO any member of the mob – a popular name for the Mafia – could be sentenced to twenty years' imprisonment and fined $25,000 if they had committed any two of 27 federal and eight state crimes, which included murder, gambling, extortion, kidnapping, bribery, robbery, drug trafficking, counterfeiting, fraud, embezzlement, money laundering and arson. Convictions for these crimes served as evidence for a new crime – racketeering to benefit an illegal enterprise.

Individuals harmed by these criminal enterprises could collect triple damages and those charged under RICO laws could be placed under a restraining order to seize their assets to prevent their dispersal.

These harsh new laws have put many of the old-style Mafia bosses away for good and have done much to impoverish the mob. However, there are always young mobsters waiting to fill the shoes of the older generation and there are always fresh rackets they can get into. As retired FBI agent David W. Breen says: 'They're like the Chinese army – you kill one and there are ten others to take his place.'

Defendants wait in cages at the back of the courtroom to have their case heard in the Maxi Trial in Palermo, Sicily.

THE MAXI TRIAL

In Italy, inroads were made into the power of the Mafia by the Maxi Trial of 1986, which saw hundreds of gangsters in the dock. More were tried *in absentia* and simply went underground. Mafia wars also thinned out the ranks.

Those imprisoned were held under restrictions outlined in Article 41-bis of the Prison Administration Act. They could be held in solitary confinement, refused the use of the telephone, banned from sending or receiving money and denied visits from family members. This meant that it was impossible to go on running a criminal organization from prison. However, with the Mafia shackled, its rivals flourished, leading to the rise of the Camorra in Naples, the 'Ndrangheta in Calabria and the Sacra Corona Unita in Puglia.

Among Italians and Italian-Americans there seems to be no shortage of young men who want to live 'the life'. This means that you have pockets full of money when others are worried about paying their bills. It gives you standing in society. These days, it also means flash cars, flash suits, bling, beautiful women and fine champagne.

On the other hand you must have no scruples. You must be able to turn your hand to any form of crime, no matter what the consequences are for others. You must be willing to kill friend, foe – and innocent bystander – without a qualm and prepared to torture others to death if that is what you are told to do.

Equally you must accept that your closest associates are likely to do that to you, too. Few Mafiosi have died in their beds of natural causes. Those going into 'the life' must accept that they are going to die in a hail of bullets, or after prolonged torture at the hands of fellow mobsters, or at best will spend many years in jail. It is the price you pay. *Mafia Files* tells the stories of a number of characters who have accepted this pact with the devil.

Al Cimino

The body of Nunzio Giuliano, 57, lies in a Neapolitan street on 21 March 2005. Giuliano was reportedly an important member of the Naples Mafia, known as the Camorra.

LUPO THE WOLF

Name: *Ignazio Lupo*

Aka: *Ignazio Saietta, Lupo the Wolf*

Born: *19 March 1877, Corleone, Sicily*

Died: *13 January 1947, Brooklyn, New York*

Gang affiliation: *Morello*

Convictions: *counterfeiting, racketeering*

From the age of ten, Ignazio Lupo worked in a grocery store in Palermo, Sicily. At the tender age of 21, he shot and killed a business rival named Salvatore Morello. Although he was convicted of 'deliberate and willful murder', Lupo had already fled.

Arriving in New York in 1898, he opened a grocery store on East 72nd Street in Manhattan with a cousin named Saietta. After a brief sojourn in Brooklyn, he moved back to Manhattan where he set up a small import business on Prince Street. Across the road was a saloon owned by Giuseppe 'the Clutch Hand' Morello, another immigrant from Corleone, Sicily and head of the Morello crime family.

In 1903, Lupo married Salvatrice Terranova, half-sister to Morello. Her brothers Vincenzo and Ciro Terranova and Nicolo Morello were also part of the Morello gang. Lupo became underboss. His name – Lupo – means 'wolf' in Italian, so he became known as Lupo the Wolf. Together they became the leading Mafia family in New York City.

Lupo developed a fearsome reputation. He was the last person seen with Brooklyn grocer Giuseppe Catania, whose body was found floating in the river under the Bay Bridge with its throat cut from ear to ear. The body was badly mutilated. No warrants were issued in the case. However, the motive for the killing was traced back to a trial in Palermo some 20 years earlier where Catania's testimony had sent a number of men to jail for 20 years.

THE BODY IN THE BARREL

The next year, the body of a man with 17 stab wounds was found stuffed in a barrel in a vacant lot near Little Italy on Manhattan's Lower East Side. His throat had been

An alley called 'Bandits' Roost' in Manhattan's Little Italy around the turn of the 20th century.
This area of the city was notoriously dilapidated and dangerous – a breeding ground for crime.

cut so savagely that his head was nearly severed from his body. His genitals had also been cut off and stuffed in his mouth. To Homicide Detective Sergeant Giuseppe 'Joe' Petrosino, later head of New York Police Department's special Italian Squad, this was all too reminiscent of Catania's murder.

The body in the barrel was not immediately identified, but Petrosino believed that he had seen the victim at the trial of counterfeiter Giuseppe De Priemo. The detective travelled to Sing Sing to see him. When shown a photograph of the dead man, De Priemo immediately identified him as his brother-in-law Benedetto Madonia. He had recently visited De Priemo with a man named Tomasso Petto – better known as 'Petto the Ox', enforcer with the Morello gang.

It seemed that Madonia had been a member of a counterfeit ring and had been murdered when money had gone missing. Petrosino rounded up the Morello gang. A search of Lupo's apartment revealed a dagger and three pistols.

The charges against most of the gang were dismissed due to lack of evidence. Only Petto was charged with murder, but went free after Madonia's wife, son, and brother-in-law refused to testify against him. Two years later, Petto was found dead outside his home with 62 stab wounds in his body.

Lupo was rearrested on counterfeiting charges, but these too were eventually dropped. In January 1904, he was arrested for carrying a concealed weapon described as 'a big blue barreled revolver of the latest kind'. Later that year, he was arrested for the kidnapping of Antonio Bozzuffi, the son of wealthy Italian banker John Bozzuffi who had previously had dealings with the Morello gang. However, brought face to face with Lupo in court, Antonio Bozzuffi said he did not recognize him.

THE WOLF VANISHES

In December 1908, Lupo's business went bankrupt in suspicious circumstances and he disappeared along with Antonio Passananti, another member of the Morello gang who had paid Lupo large sums of money while running his wholesale wine business into the ground. When the wine importer Salvatore Manzella then went bankrupt, he claimed his business had collapsed because Lupo had been

Lupo had been extorting large amounts from Manzella, who had been afraid for his life

extorting large amounts from him over the previous three years. Manzella had been afraid for his life if he did not keep paying up.

Lupo hid out under the name Joseph La Presti in upstate New York, not far from the farm of Morello-gang forger Salvatore Cina. After moving back to Brooklyn, Lupo walked into the receiver's office with his attorney

*With a shotgun wrapped in a towel, Vito Corleone (Robert De Niro) eliminates the much-feared Don Fanucci in **The Godfather, Part II**. The character of New York racketeer Don Fanucci, who terrorizes the inhabitants of Little Italy in the movie, was loosely based on Lupo the Wolf.*

and claimed that his business had failed because he had been blackmailed. He was arrested for extortion in the Manzella case, but was released when Manzella failed to appear at his arraignment. Lupo was then immediately rearrested for counterfeiting.

In 1909 Giuseppe Morello and Ignazio Saietta were sentenced to 30 years for counterfeiting and 12 smaller fry were sentenced to shorter terms. The $2 and $5 bills that had been printed in Salerno had been shipped over to New York in boxes that supposedly contained olive oil, cheese, wine, macaroni, spaghetti and other prime Italian produce. They were sold for 30 or 40 cents apiece to agents who then distributed them round the country. Both Lupo and Morello were paroled in 1920, just in time to benefit from the opportunities offered by Prohibition.

Detective Lieutenant Giuseppe 'Joe' Petrosino

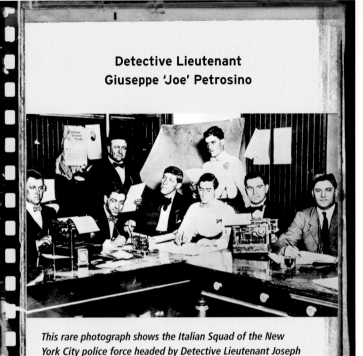

This rare photograph shows the Italian Squad of the New York City police force headed by Detective Lieutenant Joseph Petrosino (standing, left, with derby).

Born in 1860 in Salerno, southern Italy, Giuseppe Petrosino was sent to live with his grandfather in New York at the age of 14, but when his grandfather was killed in a streetcar accident, the judge in the Orphans' Court took the boy in.

In 1883, Petrosino joined the NYPD where he was befriended by Theodore Roosevelt, then police commissioner. Roosevelt promoted him to detective sergeant and Petrosino subsequently became the first Italian-American head of the Homicide Division. In this position he came up against the Black Hand gangs, Mafiosi and Camorristi who murdered those who would not succumb to their extortion. He came to public attention over the Morello barrel murder.

In an attempt to wipe out the Black Hand gangs, Petrosino was promoted to lieutenant to head the newly formed Italian Squad. Hailed as the 'Italian Sherlock Holmes', he headed to Italy to dig out the criminal records of Black Hand suspects in the United States. But his departure was carried in the newspapers and the Mafia knew he was coming. On 11 March 1909, he was shot dead in Palermo. The killer was thought to be Vito Cascio Ferro, an associate of the Morello gang and a suspect in the barrel murder case. Ferro had returned to Sicily shortly before Petrosino's arrival. News of Petrosino's assassination caused a sensation in New York. His body was shipped back to Manhattan, where an estimated 250,000 people turned out for his funeral.

THE TEFLON DON

Name: *John Gotti*

Aka: *the Teflon Don, the Dapper Don*

Born: *27 October 1940, The Bronx, New York*

Died: *10 June 2002, US Medical Center for Federal Prisoners, Springfield, Missouri*

Family affiliation: *Gambino*

Convictions: *murder, conspiracy to commit murder, loan-sharking, racketeering, obstruction of justice, illegal gambling, tax evasion, hijacking, cargo theft*

Born to a family of Italian immigrants, Gotti was one of 13 children, five of whom became made men in the Gambino family. When he was ten, Gotti's family moved to Sheepshead Bay, Brooklyn. From an early age, his ambition was to become one of the wiseguys he saw on the streets. By 12, he was running with a local street gang. At 14, while trying to steal a cement mixer, he crushed his toes, an accident which left him with a permanent limp.

A perpetual truant, Gotti dropped out of school for good at 16. Between 1957 and 1961, as a member of the Fulton-Rockaway Boys, he was arrested five times, but the charges were dismissed or reduced, so he only served probation.

Married in 1962, he took legitimate jobs as a presser in a coat factory and a truck driver's assistant. The following year, he was jailed for 20 days for auto theft. Charges of petty larceny, unlawful entry, and possession of bookmaking records followed. In 1966, he returned to jail for attempted theft.

That year he became an associate of a Mafia crew working out of the Bergin Hunt and Fish Club in Ozone Park, Queens, who targeted JFK Airport by carrying out truck hijackings.

LIFE OF CRIME

In 1967, Gotti was arrested after driving out of United Airlines' cargo area with $30,000-worth of women's clothing. While out on bail he was arrested again for

From an early age, his ambition was to become one of the wiseguys he saw on the streets

hijacking a truck carrying cigarettes worth $500,000 on the New Jersey Turnpike. He served fewer than three years in the federal penitentiary in Lewisburg, Pennsylania.

On his release, he went to work for his father-in-law's construction company and returned to the Bergin crew where he became acting *capo* at the age of 31. He reported to Gambino underboss Aniello Dellacroce at the Ravenite Social Club in Manhattan's Little Italy. When Dellacroce was jailed for tax evasion, Gotti moved up, taking orders directly from family boss Carlo Gambino.

In March 1970, flanked by FBI agents, Carlo Gambino, 67, reputed to be the Mafia's 'Boss of all Bosses', was led from FBI headquarters after his arrest for plotting to rob the crew of an armoured car containing $6 million.

When Carlo's nephew Manny Gambino was kidnapped and killed, Gotti was part of the hit team which took out Jimmy McBratney, thought to be responsible. After a plea bargain, Gotti was sentenced to four years for attempted manslaughter. Released after two, he became a made man of the Gambino family, now under the leadership of Paul Castellano.

In 1990, John Gotti (centre), wearing a trademark stylish overcoat, is led into the New York court where he was acquitted on charges of shooting a union leader.

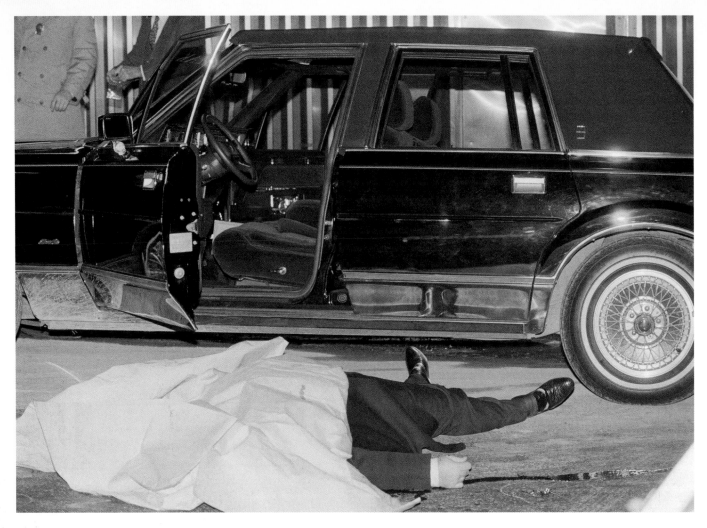

Thomas Bilotti, underboss to 'Big Paul' Castellano of the Gambino crime family, lies by his car after being gunned down outside Sparks Steak House in Manhattan. Castellano was also murdered during the hit, which was ordered by Gotti and 'Sammy the Bull' Gravano.

When Gotti's 12-year-old son Frank was accidentally run over and killed by neighbour John Favara, Favara disappeared, presumed murdered. In 1984, Gotti was charged with assault and robbery after an altercation with refrigerator mechanic Romual Piekcyk. The following year, he was indicted for racketeering. One of his co-defendants, 'Willie Boy' Johnson, turned out to be an FBI informant.

When Castellano was indicted for racketeering and other charges, he appointed Gotti acting boss, alongside Thomas Bilotti. Then Castellano discovered that Gotti was involved in narcotics, against Gambino policy. When Dellacroce died, Bilotti became underboss. This was considered a slight by Gotti and the Dellacroce family.

On 16 December 1985, Castellano was shot dead outside Sparks Steak House in Manhattan while Gotti and Salvatore 'Sammy the Bull' Gravano watched from their car. In front of a street full of Christmas shoppers, hitman Tony 'Roach' Rampino also pumped six shots into Bilotti, who was chauffeuring Castellano. Following the hit, Gotti took over as head of the Gambino family with Gravano as underboss.

'I FORGOTTI'

Unlike other gangsters, Gotti did not shy away from the public eye. The 'Dapper Don' was always immaculately turned out. A celebrity gangster, he appeared to be above the law. At Gotti's trial for felony and assault in March 1986, the complainant Romual Piekcyk said that he could not see his attackers in the courtroom. When asked to describe the men who had assaulted him, he said: 'To be perfectly honest, it is so long ago I don't remember' – prompting the famous *New York Daily News* headline: 'I FORGOTTI'.

Piekcyk was declared a hostile witness and the charges against Gotti were dismissed.

Two weeks later, after a vacation in Florida, Gotti was back in court on racketeering charges. Standing trial alongside him were his younger brother Gene and five other members of the Gambino family. Not present was Aniello Dellacroce's son, Armond, who had also been indicted in the federal investigation into the Mafia Commission. Four days after his father's death he pleaded guilty to racketeering and conspiracy charges, contravening Gotti's instructions that no member should admit that the Gambino family even existed. Frightened for his life, Armond Dellacroce disappeared before sentencing. in the Pocono Mountains of Pennsylvania, he died of a cerebral haemorrhage brought on by alcohol poisoning, as the police closed in.

With Aniello Dellacroce dead, Gotti was the chief defendant. He was charged with seven 'predicate acts' – that is, crimes committed to further an illegal enterprise. Three of these were crimes he had already served time for: two hijackings and the killing of James McBratney. Under the RICO laws, the McBratney manslaughter was elevated to murder.

Bringing the charges, the assistant US Attorney Diana Giacalone took seven months to present the evidence, which included the testimony of almost a hundred witnesses and 30 hours of taped conversations. But Gotti's defence attorney, Bruce Cutler – himself a former assistant DA – claimed that the taped conversations were innocent and some of the witnesses were confessed criminals, murderers and kidnappers who had benefited by getting lighter sentences for giving testimony. They were hardly credible, he argued. Besides, wasn't it double jeopardy to punish someone again for crimes they had already done time for? Gotti was acquitted. He returned to Ozone Park where yellow ribbons had been tied around the trees. The press were now calling him 'the Teflon Don' because nothing seemed to stick.

Indeed an indictment for shooting union official John O'Connor failed to stick, too. Instead, as boss of the United Brotherhood of Carpenters and Joiners of America, O'Connor himself was convicted of racketeering.

On 24 January 1989, defence attorney Bruce Cutler (left) gestures broadly during the arraignment of John Gotti, his client. With two associates, Gotti was charged with first-degree assault in the May 1986 shooting of New York City union leader, John O'Connor.

ABOVE RETRIBUTION

While Gotti was immune to the law, he also seemed above retribution from the mob itself. When Vincent 'the Chin' Gigante, head of the Genovese family, ordered a hit on him, the FBI warned Gotti. He was therefore on his guard and the killers only managed to assassinate Gotti's underboss, Frank DeCicco.

With others in jail on RICO charges, Gotti promoted Gravano to underboss. He was also kicking back around $100,000 a month from the construction industry. Although younger Mafiosi were attracted to Gotti's flashy suits, his high profile was also attracting the attention of the FBI. They prepared a new RICO case, based around the murder of Castellano. When FBI

> **The Teflon is gone. The don is covered with Velcro, and all charges stick**

agents managed to plant a bug in the apartment above the Ravenite Social Club – Gotti's new headquarters – Gotti was caught on tape discussing murder and other crimes. One soldier, they heard, had been 'whacked' when he did not come quickly enough when he was called. Another had been killed because Gravano said he had talked about Gotti behind his back. Gotti trusted Gravano to the point that he designated him acting

On 15 June 2002, pallbearers carry the casket of John Gotti from the Papavero Funeral Home to a waiting hearse on Grand Avenue after a funeral service in Maspeth, Queens.

boss if Gotti was taken off the streets. Meanwhile Frank LoCascio took over as acting *consigliere*.

In December 1990, Gotti, Gravano and LoCascio were indicted for criminal enterprise, obstruction of justice, income-tax evasion, loan-sharking, illegal gambling and four counts of murder. They were denied bail, so Gotti's son, John Gotti Jr., took over the day-to-day running of the organization.

Although Gravano had been a mobster since his twenties – first indicted for murder in 1974 – he had never served time before. Prisons used to be run by mobsters, almost as retirement homes. But by 1990 they were being run by African-Americans – and Italian-Americans were definitely second-class citizens.

Gravano heard that Gotti was saying he had played the peaceful boss who spent his time restraining Gravano, who was a 'mad dog' killer. Eventually Gravano turned state's evidence in return for a reduced sentence. He admitted to having been involved in 19 murders, ten of which Gotti had ordered. These included the murders of Castellano and Bilotti. Nevertheless Gotti still thought he would walk. But the jury returned 13 guilty verdicts. Gotti was sentenced to five life terms – four without parole – plus 65 years and a fine of $250,000.

He was incarcerated in the federal penitentiary at Marion, Illinois – reputed to be one of the toughest prisons in the United States. After being beaten up by a fellow inmate, he effectively spent the rest of his life in solitary confinement, only leaving his cell for one hour a day. He died of throat cancer in 2002.

Gravano was sentenced to five years, but after the time he had already done was taken into consideration, he served only one. On his release, he moved to Phoenix, Arizona, where he was rearrested in 2000. The following year, he pleaded guilty to drug trafficking charges and was sentenced to another 20 years.

John Favara

Furniture warehouse manager John Favara lived on the next block to John Gotti in the Howard Beach area of Queens, New York. His adopted son Scott was a friend of Gotti's children and Favara had a close friend who had joined the mob.

On 18 March 1980, 12-year-old Frank Gotti was killed when he darted out from behind a dumpster on a motorized minibike and was hit by Favara's car. Favara told the police he had been momentarily blinded by the sun. Investigators accepted that the crash was an accident and no charges were brought.

When Favara went to apologize to Frank's mother, Victoria Gotti, she attacked him with a baseball bat. For months he was subjected to harassment and death threats, and the word 'murderer' was spray-painted on his car.

On 28 July, three days before he was due to move away from Howard Beach, Favara was grabbed while he was leaving work and thrown into a van. Neither Favara nor his car were seen again. The police were told that Gotti had cut up Favara with a chainsaw while he was still alive. The dead man's remains were stuffed in a barrel of concrete and thrown off a pier in Sheepshead Bay. When questioned, Gotti said: 'I'm not sorry the guy's missing. I wouldn't be sorry if the guy turned up dead.'

It is now believed that John Favara was shot dead by hitman Charles Carneglia and his body was dissolved in acid.

THE TEACHER

Name: *Antonietta (Ninetta) Riina née Bagarella*

Born: *1944, Corleone, Sicily*

Gang affiliation: *Leggio*

Indictment: *accomplice of Mafia boss Totò Riina, criminal association*

Ninetta Bagarella was born into a Mafia family. From 1963 to 1968, her father Salvatore Bagarella had lived in exile in northern Italy because of his involvement with the Mafia. Her eldest brother Giuseppe was also sent into exile and was murdered in prison in 1972. The next eldest, Calogero, was a childhood friend of Bernardo Provenzano and Salvatore 'Totò' Riina.

At the age of 12, Totò Riina effectively became head of the family while his father Giovanni Riina was emptying the explosives from a wartime shell, so he could sell the metal casing as scrap. The shell slipped from Giovanni's grasp and exploded, killing him and one of his sons, seven-year-old Francesco, and wounding another son, Gaetano. Only Totò was left unhurt.

YOUNG MAFIA RECRUIT

Unrestrained by the firm hand of a father, Totò soon turned his back on the life of a peasant and hung about in the piazza of Corleone, telling his friends that he was not going to die poor. He and Provenzano were recruited by Luciano Leggio, hitman for the local doctor and *capomafia* Michele Navarra. The three of them did a brisk trade in stealing cattle and selling the butchered meat. They would greet each other with a kiss on the cheek, a typical Mafia gesture. Riina was warned off joining the Mafia by a local policeman, Provenzano by an older brother. It did no good.

In May 1949, after the procession of the crucified Christ in Corleone, Riina and his friends got into a fight with Domenico Di Matteo using sticks and knuckle-dusters. Ten days later there was another fight outside town. This time it ended with gunfire. Riina loosed off half-a-dozen shots with an automatic. One shot fatally wounded Di Matteo and Riina himself was wounded. He was arrested in his hospital bed.

In court, in chains, he spoke abusively to the judge and was sentenced to 12 years. He served only six.

TRADITIONAL COURTSHIP

The year after Riina's release, he was invited to stay for dinner at the home of his friend Calogero Bagarella.

Calogero's sister, 13-year-old Ninetta, served at table. Although at 26 Totò was twice her age, he was instantly smitten with her pretty oval face, black eyes and long black hair, which she wore in a ponytail.

For Riina, her family background could not have been better – by then a third brother had joined the Mafia. What's more, Calogero was in love with Riina's sister. But Ninetta was something special. While Riina was barely literate, Ninetta was an avid reader, improving her mind by poring over books from the school library. She sat in the front row in class and studied Latin and Greek. A model pupil, she saw education as a way of escaping poverty and she was determined to get a proper job when she grew up.

She also consumed novels to give herself a broader perspective. The ones she picked usually concerned the

From the 1960s onwards, the town of Corleone became infamous for Mafia activities.

plight of the oppressed and poor and their struggle against their oppressors.

'What I read in those books,' she said, 'was life in Corleone.'

She was also fascinated by Machiavelli – 'because his principle, the end justifies the means, was applied to the letter by the local police,' she said.

Despite this intellectual rift between them, Riina wooed Ninetta in the traditional way. Every morning he would wait in the narrow alleyway where she lived and follow her to school. On the way, not a word was spoken.

'For years I followed her with my eyes, for years I never gave her a moment's rest,' he said, 'until she decided to marry me.'

DEADLY FEUD

Meanwhile a feud had broken out between Leggio and Navarra, who had vetoed a lucrative construction project Leggio was involved in. Leggio then put the squeeze on one of Navarra's lieutenants. Navarra arranged an ambush and Leggio was wounded in the arm. Honour had been satisfied, or so Navarra thought. He was wrong.

On 2 August 1958, Navarra was being driven home from Lercara Friddi, birthplace of 'Lucky' Luciano, by a doctor who had no Mafia associations. Navarra was unarmed and had no bodyguard. They were ambushed by Leggio, Provenzano and Riina, who had abandoned the traditional *lupara*, or sawn-off shotgun, in favour of Al Capone-style sub-machine guns and automatic pistols. They fired 124 bullets into the car; 92 of them hit Navarra.

A month later, they made peace overtures to Navarra loyalists and Riina was sent alone and unarmed to a Mafia meeting.

'Who's dead is dead,' he said. 'The dear departed has gone away. Let us think of the living.'

Solemnly he crossed himself. Before there was an answer, Provenzano and another man appeared and

A Mafia victim, 1966; part of a long history of violence in Sicily.

opened fire with sawn-off shotguns. One of Navarra's men was shot in the face. The others fled.

In the ensuing chase through the streets of Corleone, a two-year-old girl was wounded by a stray bullet. Provenzano was hit in the head and left for dead. Two women were injured, along with an eight-year-old girl. But when the police arrived, no one had seen anything. Interviewed in his hospital bed, Provenzano claimed to have been on his way to the cinema when he collapsed unconscious.

'I have no idea what happened,' he said.

SILENT WAR

War broke out and Riina quickly became one of Leggio's most trusted killers, never hesitating to cut down Navarra loyalists and any inconvenient witnesses. The final shot was always to the mouth, to warn anyone who knew anything to remain silent. The *omertà*, or code of silence, was absolute. A journalist asked a weeping mother walking behind a coffin: 'Who was killed?' She replied: 'Why, is somebody dead?'

Some 50 people were murdered and there were a further 22 murder attempts. At first, victims were shot down in the streets, shops and bars, or in their homes. Then came the *lupara bianca* or 'white shotgun'. People simply disappeared, their bodies thrown down ravines, dissolved in lime or burnt on giant grills over open fires.

Provenzano was wounded trying to ambush Navarra lieutenant Francesco Paolo Streva in the alleyway where Ninetta lived. As he made his escape, a woman emerged to wipe up the trail of blood. Streva was ambushed again four months later. This time he was murdered and left in a ditch, together with his two bodyguards and their guard dog. Leggio and his two lieutenants, Provenzano and Riina, were now in control in Corleone.

But this was not enough for Leggio. He wanted to move into Palermo. The move prompted another Mafia war. It became so ferocious that Leggio and his men had to go into hiding.

In December 1963, Riina was caught in a police roadblock. He found himself in the Ucciardone prison in Palermo, surrounded by incarcerated Palermo dons wearing silk dressing gowns and brandishing silver cigarette holders. They looked down on the Corleonesi – which only fuelled Riina's ambition further.

'When I get out of here,' he said, 'I want to walk on a carpet of 100,000-lire banknotes.'

Six months after Riina's capture, Leggio was arrested. Provenzano was picked up as well. All three refused to co-operate with the authorities and in 1969 they appeared in the dock together in Bari along with another 61 Mafiosi. Due to the intimidation of the jury, they were all acquitted. Riina was only found guilty of stealing a driving licence and was sentenced to six months, time he had already served.

FORMAL ENGAGEMENT

Riina returned to Corleone, where he was rearrested and sentenced to four years' exile. He was granted a few days' liberty to settle his domestic affairs and he used the time to formalize his engagement to Ninetta, who was by now a 26-year-old teacher. While he had been away she had enrolled at Palermo University, to study literature and philosophy. Travelling there by bus every day, she was accompanied by two police officers who suspected she had links to the Mafia. Then two of her brothers shot a cattle breeder who was wooing her sister. One brother was arrested and the other went on the run. Ninetta was forced to give up her studies. Instead, she took a teaching post in a private institute.

Riina took his mother to meet Ninetta's mother. The two women would formally seek 'clarification' – that is, discuss the dowry and make arrangements for where the couple would live. The dowry was small. Riina was not

I am guilty only of loving a man who I esteem and trust

a rich man, but Ninetta's mother was confident that he could make money, provided he stayed out of jail.

Business concluded, drinks were served and Riina gave Ninetta the ring.

'We got engaged in the intimacy of our families,' said Ninetta. 'It's not as if we said to each other "I love you" or "You're the light of my life". We were serious people.'

Riina then went into exile in San Giovanni in Persiceto, near Bologna in northern Italy. He signed in at the police station there, but disappeared a few days later to become a fugitive again.

Meanwhile, Ninetta's brother Calogero Bagarella joined Provenzano in Leggio's hit squad to take out Michele 'the Cobra' Cavataio in the ongoing Palermo war. Dressed in police uniforms, they shot up Cavataio's headquarters. Calogero Bagarella was shot and fatally wounded. Provenzano was wounded too, but he finished the job with a machine gun. When it jammed, he hit Cavataio's skull with the butt until it caved in. Riina made a brief appearance in public at Calogero's funeral.

Leggio was in poor health, so Riina and Provenzano went to work for the *capomafia* of Cinisi, Gaetano Badalamenti and Stefano 'the Prince' Bontate, another *capo* in Palermo. Riina seized the opportunity to learn as much as he could about the inside workings of the Sicilian Mafia. It stood him in good stead.

When Leggio moved to Milan, Riina became his representative on the Mafia triumvirate, whose other members were Badalamenti and Bontate. But Bontate mocked him for being a peasant and tried to get him

Palermo is the economic hub of Sicily and has therefore been an important centre for the Mafia.

arrested. Nevertheless Riina took his place on the broader Commission that replaced the triumvirate.

ON TRIAL FOR LOVE

In July 1971, Ninetta Bagarella arrived at the law courts in Palermo. The 27-year-old schoolteacher looked nothing like a Mafia wife. Eschewing austere black clothing, she wore a blue dress with yellow and red flowers printed on it, the hemline above the knee, high-heeled shoes and her diamond engagement ring. She had been accused of being the liaison between the Leggio clan and several fugitives. The police had evidence that she had arranged Leggio's various stays in hospital.

The year before, the police had requested her passport. She sent it to them, together with a letter calling them 'persecutors, tormentors, torturers'. This brought a charge of slander. The police then brought about her dismissal from the school in which she had taught physical education for four years. They now sought to have her exiled to the mainland. She was the first woman they had tried to banish.

Ninetta brought with her a petition drawn up by the archpriest of Corleone, a colleague of Ninetta's at school, and signed by scores of residents. In it, the archpriest said that the Bagarellas were 'an exemplary family dogged by misfortune and the law that does not respect the affairs of the heart and persecutes a schoolteacher just because she is engaged to Salvatore Riina'.

Of Ninetta's 'exemplary family', a father and brother were in exile; another brother was officially a fugitive but had actually been gunned down in a hit two years earlier; and a third brother was Riina's lieutenant.

However, the archpriest said: 'Her mother comes to Mass every morning and takes communion.'

In court, the presiding judge said: 'Miss Bagarella, you know it has been proposed that you be sent into exile.'

In a clear, calm voice, Ninetta replied: 'I don't believe the court wants to send me into exile. If you have a conscience, if you have a heart, you won't do it. Only the women remain in our family. We have to work for ourselves and for our men, father and brothers who have been dogged by misfortune. I am a woman and I am guilty only of loving a man who I esteem and trust. I have always loved Totò Riina. I was 13 and he was 26 when I first fell in love. He has never been out of my heart. That is all I am guilty of, your honour.'

The judge pointed out that Riina was a dangerous criminal who was wanted for numerous murders.

Ninetta dismissed this: 'A pack of lies. Slander. Salvatore is innocent.'

She was then accused of belonging to the Leggio clan. 'I don't even know Leggio,' she said.

For over an hour she parried every accusation thrown at her. Her lawyer then delivered dozens of testimonials from fellow teachers, pupils and parents.

'The only thing I want is to marry Riina,' she told the court. 'I don't want our relationship to remain platonic. But I have not seen him for such a long time. I know nothing about him. I don't even know if he still loves me.'

The judge denied the petition to send her to the mainland, but ordered that she be put under police surveillance for two-and-a-half years. She was also placed under curfew from 7.30 pm to 7 am.

After the hearing, she was asked by a journalist:

Ninetta on Riina

Before her trial in Palermo, Ninetta gave an interview to the newspaper *Giornale di Sicilia* in an office near the courtroom.

'I am nervous, very nervous,' she said, 'even if I am making an effort to remain calm to put my case to the judges. The flashes of the photographers' cameras don't help keep me calm. I don't like publicity,' she said.

She was unapologetic about her love for Riina.

'You think bad of me because I, a teacher, have fallen for and become engaged to a man like Salvatore Riina,' she said. 'But I am a woman. Don't I have the right to love a man and follow the pull of nature? I picked him firstly because I loved him and love ignores many things, and then because I admire and trust him. I love Riina because I believe he is innocent. . . . I am here for him today. He has been away from me for two years. I haven't heard anything from him directly or indirectly. I am a woman and this makes me doubt his love. I feel alone and disheartened. . . . Riina does not care about the feelings or needs of a woman.'

In court, she said the only thing she was guilty of was loving Totò Riina, Mafia boss and multiple murderer.

'What is the Mafia?'

'The Mafia is a phenomenon created by the newspapers to sell more newspapers,' she shot back.

Hearing of her testimony, Riina said: 'I don't want any other woman. I only want Ninetta. They don't want me to marry her? Well, I will carry out a massacre.'

Tommaso Buscetta in court; in 1986 scores of Mafia suspects were convicted on evidence supplied by Buscetta.

MARRIED ON THE RUN

Just one week before the end of her sentence, a policeman visited the Bagarella household after 7.30 pm. Ninetta was not there. The policeman was told that Ninetta had got a job in Germany. In fact, she was with Riina. Now both of them were on the run. Nevertheless they were married by Mafioso priest Father Agostino Coppola, nephew of Frank 'Three Fingers' Coppola, a leading light of the Gambino family, though the marriage was never registered. The couple spent their honeymoon in Venice. Nine months later, Ninetta gave birth to their first child, a daughter named Concetta, in an exclusive clinic in Palermo. She gave birth to three more children there – Giovanni, Giuseppe and Lucia. She registered them under her own name and neither she nor Riina, who visited, was bothered by the police.

In 1974, Leggio was jailed for the murder of Navarra, and Riina took over the Corleonesi. He sought to dominate the heroin trade and ordered hits on a number of the policemen, judges and prosecutors who tried to stop him. Snooping reporters were unwelcome too. In 1979, Ninetta's brother Leoluca killed Mario Francese, a journalist on the *Giornale di Sicilia*. Then a fresh Mafia war broke out in Sicily.

Riina and Ninetta moved into a villa in Palermo with a damp-proof underground vault to store her furs. Although she had over a million dollars' worth of jewellery, she could not visit her mother. Her children had to be escorted to school and, according to her sisters, she was reprimanded by Riina for standing on the balcony.

BOSS OF BOSSES

In 1983, convicted killer Tommaso Buscetta, who had been on the losing side in the war, became a *pentito*, that is a 'penitent one' who turns state's evidence – the first senior Mafia figure to do so. He revealed that the Mafia was a single organization run by a Commission, or *Cupola*, headed by Riina. To divert resources from the investigation Riina organized a terrorist-style attack, known as the Christmas Massacre, in 1984. A bomb was detonated in a tunnel through the Apennines between Florence and Bologna, killing 17 and injuring 267. Nevertheless, Buscetta's evidence led to the Maxi Trial in 1986, which led to the conviction of 338 Mafiosi. Riina was given a life sentence *in absentia*.

He continued his campaign of murdering rivals to maintain his position as 'boss of bosses', while simultaneously cultivating political connections. When the Maxi Trial convictions were upheld, Riina ordered the assassination of the former mayor of Palermo Salvatore Lima, along with prosecuting magistrates Giovanni Falcone and Paolo Borsellino.

The killing of Falcone and Borsellino led to public outrage. Fearing the wrath of Riina, the acting boss of the San Giuseppe clan, Balduccio Di Maggio, fled Sicily and became a *pentito*. He told the authorities he had a rough idea of where Riina lived. Studying footage of film shot covertly in the area, he spotted Ninetta getting into a car. Next day, Riina was arrested coming out of the same building.

Although Provenzano became titular head of the Corleonesi, it was thought that the faction was run by Ninetta's brother Leoluca until his arrest in 1995. Two years later, Riina's son Giovanni was arrested. Ninetta wrote an open letter to the Rome newspaper *La Repubblica*, saying: 'I've decided to open my heart, which is swollen and overflowing with sadness for the arrest of my son Giovanni. . . . At home we all miss him, our family situation has become hell, we cannot accept that a boy barely 20 years old, with no previous convictions, is first arrested, then questioned for two days and then jailed.'

Ninetta appealed to the mayor of Corleone for help. While intimidated by her presence, there was nothing he could do. In 2001, Giovanni was sentenced to life imprisonment for four murders. The following year, his younger brother Giuseppe was given 14 years for extortion, money laundering and criminal association. Then in 2007 the widow of Paolo Borsellino filed a civil suit for damages against Ninetta and was awarded €3,360,000 compensation.

Ninetta Bagarella on her daughter's wedding day in 2008

LITTLE DOLL

Name: *Assunta Maresca*

Aka: *Pupetta (Little Doll)*

Born: *19 January 1935, Castellammare di Stabia, Naples, Italy*

Gang affiliation: *Lampetielli (Lightning Flashes)*

Convictions: *murder, extortion*

Assunta Maresca was the only daughter of Camorrista Vincenzo Maresca, whose family, the Lampetielli – known for their lightning speed with flick knives and pistols – controlled Castellammare di Stabia, a small town to the south of Naples. Pretty and spoilt, she earned the nickname *Pupetta*, or 'Little Doll'.

She was renowned for her beauty and was jealously guarded by her four brothers, who beat her if she so much as caught a man's eye. Nevertheless, she entered a beauty contest and became 'Miss Rovegliano'. And when an old-style *guappo*, or Camorra boss, who was ten years her senior – Pasquale Simonetti aka Pascalone 'e Nola (Big Pasquale of Nola) – began courting the buxom 17-year-old, her brothers acquiesced.

When they married in 1955, the whole town turned out. There were five hundred guests at the wedding breakfast. They brought envelopes stuffed with money or jewels for the princess.

WIDOWED AND PREGNANT

With her marriage, Pupetta acquired a new status. In the morning, people queued outside her house, bringing gifts of cheese or wine. If a son had been arrested, Simonetti would be asked if he could find a good lawyer. If a girl had been dumped by her boyfriend, could he buy her some furniture to act as a dowry? Simonetti was there as an arbiter. Traditionally he would summon a boy who had

The wedding of racketeer Pasquale Simonetti and beauty queen Pupetta Maresca in 1955. After a few months, Pasquale was killed. A short time later Antonio Esposito lay dead when Pupetta took her revenge on the man who had ordered the killing.

seduced and abandoned a local girl and give him a wad of money. 'This is for your wedding or your funeral – you decide,' he would say.

Simonetti made his money from smuggling cigarettes and was reputed to have slapped Lucky Luciano. From Nola, a town ten miles inland from Naples, Simonetti also fixed the price of fruit and vegetables in the city. Another contender was Antonio Esposito, who had ordered a hit on Simonetti.

One day in the marketplace, Simonetti was approached by a man who was called 'the Ship' because of his rolling gait. He went for his gun, but the Ship was too fast for

him. After being hit in the stomach Simonetti was taken to hospital, but he told the police nothing. Pupetta rushed to his bedside to find him bleeding heavily.

'I begged him to tell me what had happened,' she said. 'He told me Esposito was behind it. . . . That's how I knew who did it.'

Simonetti survived the night, but died the following morning, leaving Pupetta a widow at 20. She was pregnant at the time. Afraid that she might also be on Esposito's hit list, she moved back in with her parents.

'I was frightened in the house on my own,' she said. 'It was like a nightmare, after starting a new life with my

I fired the first shot.
He was going to kill me

handsome prince, to be back living with my mother.'

She told the police that Esposito was responsible, but they did nothing. She had no proof. No one in the market had seen anything apparently, or perhaps they were suffering a convenient lapse of memory. However, if Simonetti's murder went unpunished, it would diminish her status as the widow of an important man.

WOMAN OF HONOUR

Esposito began sending her threatening messages. It seemed that he knew her every move, so she began carrying her husband's gun – a Smith & Wesson .38 – which she had taken from his bedside as a 'memento'.

She was making her daily visit to the cemetery, accompanied by her driver and her 13-year-old brother, when she saw Esposito walking along the road. She stopped the car. Esposito strolled up and said: 'I hear you have been looking for me.'

He reached in the window and chucked her under the chin.

'Here I am,' he said. 'Get out of the car.'

He tried to open the door, but Pupetta reached into her handbag and pulled out Pasquale's gun. Holding it in both hands, she opened fire.

'I fired the first shot,' she admitted. 'He was going to kill me.'

Twenty-nine bullets were found in Esposito's body and Pupetta's brother disappeared.

While awaiting trial, she gave birth to a son, Pasqualino – 'Little Pasquale' – in jail. She wrote reassuringly to her parents: 'Think of me as a girl away at college,' she said.

'Sometimes I laugh and sing.'

While in jail, she was bombarded with proposals of marriage. Inspired by her example, a musician composed a song called '*La Legge d'Onore*' – 'The Law of Honour' – and the newspapers called her 'The Diva of Crime'.

Flowers were showered from the balconies on to the police van carrying her to court. For the first time, microphones were allowed in the courtrooms of Naples Assizes so the crowd could hear what was going on.

While no witnesses could be found for the murder of Simonetti, 85 turned out for Pupetta's trial. She was unrepentant, telling the court: 'I would do it again.' With that, the court erupted with cheers.

Pupetta was found guilty and sentenced to 14 years.

'Prison was a nightmare,' she said. 'It was run by nuns, wizened old hags who were consumed with envy. I was young. I had just got married. I had my lovely silk underwear . . . they took it away and gave me a rough sack dress to wear, shapeless and several sizes too big. I threw it back at them. "You wear it!" I said.'

She did her best to give the nuns hell, refusing to have her hair cut and demanding to see the governor.

'You can imagine me in the midst of all those old women rotting in jail. There were some young ones too, but they were from Calabria and Sicily – primitive girls.'

Having proved herself to be 'a woman of honour', she inherited her husband's authority. Other prisoners waited on her, bringing her clean bed linen and hot coffee and asking her for favours. She had food brought in for those less fortunate and stuck up for inmates' rights, effectively becoming the boss of the prison and earning the nickname 'Madame Camorra'.

She was allowed to keep her son with her until he was three. Then he was sent to be brought up by her mother. When she was released at the age of 31, her son was a stranger to her.

KILLED BY HIS MOTHER'S LOVER?

A former cellmate introduced Ninetta to handsome Camorrista Umberto Ammaturo, who ran guns from Germany to Libya and cocaine from South America to Italy, via Nigeria. They became lovers and she gave birth to twins. But Ammaturo and Pasqualino did not get on.

The young man wanted to prove himself. He had already pulled a gun on the nephew of a Camorrista known simply as '*O Malommo*' – 'the Bad Man'. And he had let it be known that once he was 18 he was going to kill Gaetano Orlando – the gunman who had killed his father. In January 1974, the day after his 18th

In February 1960, among the market workers of Naples, two elegantly dressed men control the trade of pears and oranges. Like the Mafia in Sicily, the Camorra in Naples has a long history and is possibly the direct descendant of a Spanish secret society, the Garduña, founded in 1417.

birthday, Pasqualino was due to meet Ammaturo on the construction site of Naples' new flyover. He was never seen again.

Pupetta believed that Ammaturo knew something about Pasqualino's disappearance. She asked him about it repeatedly – to the point that he would beat her up for asking. If he had admitted to knowing anything about Pasqualino's death, Pupetta would have killed

> ## If Cutolo touches my family, I will have his gunmen killed . . . even the women and babies in their cradles

him. She even approached Judge Italo Ormanni, who was investigating the disappearance, telling him that Ammaturo had killed her son, but she refused to sign a formal complaint. The judge was convinced that Pasqualino's body was in one of the pillars supporting the flyover, but he failed to get permission to knock it down.

Even so, Pupetta did not leave Ammaturo and continued to help him in his criminal activities. When war broke out between Raffaele Cutolo's Nuova Camorra Organizzata and the Nuova Famiglia faction, Pupetta's favourite brother was shot several times. He survived, but was sentenced to four years in prison, where he was again threatened by Cutolo's men.

MEDIA FIGURE

In 1982, Pupetta called a press conference at the Press Club in Naples. 'If Cutolo touches one member of my family, I will have his gunmen killed,' she declared. 'I will kill his lackeys, even the women and babies in their cradles. . . . The whole region is being strangled by an invisible force, seeping through every strata of society.

Camorra boss Raffaele Cutolo, seen here in 2005, is serving multiple life sentences for murder.

That insidious force is Raffaele Cutolo. He wants to rule at any price – you are either with him or against him. Cutolo wants to become emperor of Naples, and this town is in chains because of him. All these deaths, the rivers of blood which are running through our city as people watch helplessly, all this is caused by one power-crazed madman.'

Cutolo dismissed this as histrionics. 'Pupetta should have more dignity,' he said. 'She has made a complete fool of herself.'

Behind the scenes he started threatening her.

Later that year, Pupetta and Ammaturo were arrested for extortion and the murder of forensic psychiatrist Aldo Semerari, who had helped Ammaturo escape jail by feigning insanity. His severed head was found between his legs. Ammaturo fled to South America leaving Pupetta to face the music alone. She was sentenced to four years. Maintaining her innocence, she claimed that Cutolo had used his contacts in the judiciary to put her away.

'I was tortured by the judges, every day of those four years,' she said. 'The first 14 years were different because I had committed a crime and it was right that I paid for it. But those four years in prison were terrible because there is no peace for an innocent person in prison.'

Ammaturo was later acquitted on appeal due to lack of evidence. However, when he became a *pentito* in 1993 he admitted to the murder.

After leaving prison, Pupetta retired to Sorrento. In 1988, a film, *Il caso Pupetta Maresca*, was made about her life. The title role was played by Alessandra Mussolini, granddaughter of Benito, the former Italian dictator.

In 2000, Pupetta made the newspapers again when she complained to the police that an employee had run off with the 10 billion lira – $5 million – she had won on Italy's biggest lottery. She said she had dispatched Giovanni Boscaglia, a 67-year-old small-time criminal, to play the numbers they had picked. But when they came up she did not hear from him.

However, Pupetta's contacts in the Neapolitan underworld soon tracked him down. Boscaglia agreed to go to a notary public to hand over the winning ticket and sign a legal agreement that the pair would divide the winnings. But lottery officials said the ticket he handed over was a fake.

The Manchester Mafiosa

One Sicilian godmother surprisingly hails from Rochdale, just outside Manchester, England.

In 1979, Ann Hathaway, then a 17-year-old dancer, met Antonio Rinzivillo in a club in northern Italy. They married, had two children and lived in Rome. Rinzivillo and his brother Gino specialized in arms trafficking, drug dealing and extortion for Giuseppe 'Piddu' Madonia, second-in-command to Totò Riina until his arrest in 1992.

Rinzivillo was jailed for four-and-a-half years soon after they married and was in jail for all but four of their 20-year marriage. His wife claimed that she knew nothing of his criminal activities. However, according the authorities in Sicily, she was a go-between for the Rinzivillos and their criminal network.

'She was a significant focal point through which passed all the orders and messages for other members of the organization,' said Major Bartolomeo Di Niso of the Sicilian Carabinieri. 'She was a point of contact which would keep the whole machine running.'

Hathaway was taped demanding $120,000 from Rinzivillo's money launderer, Angelo Bernascone, for her brother-in-law, Gino. In another tape, recorded a few weeks later in August 2005, she warned Bernascone of Gino's anger when he fails to pay, telling him: 'My brother-in-law was f*****g furious.'

On 1 October that year, her brother-in-law was heard on tape issuing a warning to Bernascone via Hathaway. He is heard telling her: 'You tell him "My brother-in-law has lost many friends and it's your fault . . . clearly people were right about you . . . " Tell him "You and I are through. Full stop".' Bernascone turned himself in to the police in September 2006, saying he feared he was going to be killed.

Accused of running her husband's empire while he was in jail, Hathaway was also sought.

'You can't just arrest somebody just because you're married to someone that's got problems,' she protested. 'What's that got to do with me?'

Having fled back to England, she faced extradition. In a plea bargain, she admitted associating with the Mafia and was given a two-year suspended sentence. If her husband ever gets out of jail, she hopes he will join her in Rochdale.

THE ICE MAN

Name: *Richard Kuklinski*

Born: *11 April 1935, Jersey City, New Jersey*

Died: *5 March 2006*

Gang affiliation: *DeCavalcante, Gambino*

Conviction: *six counts of murder*

Richard Kuklinski was a Mafia hit man who claimed to have killed over a hundred people. A professional assassin, he earned the soubriquet 'The Ice Man' because of his habit of refrigerating bodies to disguise the time of death.

Curiously for a Mafioso, he was not a Sicilian or an Italian. His father was Polish, his mother Irish and he was brought up in the projects of Jersey City. His father was an alcoholic who beat his children savagely for no reason. Richard's elder brother died as a result of these beatings. Kuklinski later regretted not killing his father. He actually went to a bar where his father hung out to put a bullet in his head, but he wasn't there.

Kuklinski tried to defend his mother from one of his father's beatings. This earned him a punch that put him out for half the night. But his mother beat him too, hitting him around the head with pots and pans, shoes, brushes and broom handles.

He was sent to a Catholic school where he was beaten by the priests and the nuns. Angry, he vented his rage on cats and dogs, torturing them and burning or beating them to death while enjoying their screams. Once he tied the tails of two cats together, hung them over a washing line and watched them tear each other to pieces.

TEENAGE KILLER

When his parents separated, Kuklinski supplemented the family's meagre diet by stealing. He also stole true crime

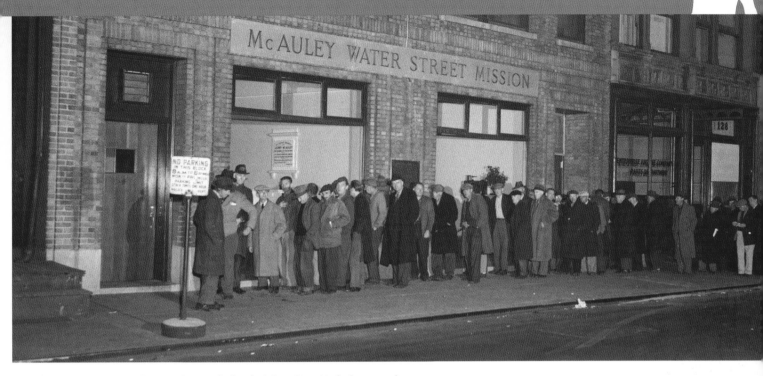

Kuklinski took perverse pleasure in murdering helpless New York down-and-outs and homosexuals.

magazines, which he studied obsessively. By the time he was 13, he had graduated to stealing cars. At 14, he committed his first murder.

Bullied by a gang headed by Charley Lane, Kuklinski beat Lane to death with a thick wooden pole. He put the body in the boot of a stolen car and dumped it in a river that ran through a vast, densely forested area known as Pine Barrens. First of all, though, he smashed the corpse's teeth and cut off its fingertips to prevent identification. Back in the Jersey City projects, Kuklinski tracked down the rest of Charley Lane's gang one by one and beat them up viciously.

After quitting school, he hung out in pool halls where he learned that you could win any fight if you struck first with full force, usually wielding a pool cue. Anyone who got the better of him was later knifed.

He formed a gang whose members were tattooed with the words 'Coming Up Roses' on their left hands – the idea being that anyone who crossed them would end up as plant food. They planned robberies and stick-ups and Kuklinski armed himself with a .38 revolver with a six-inch barrel.

When his father visited to administer another beating to his mother, he put the gun to his head and pulled back the hammer. His father did not bother the family again.

Then an Irish policeman named Doyle called Kuklinski a 'dumb Polack' in a bar. When Doyle went out to his car, Kuklinski poured petrol over it and struck a match.

PRACTISING HIS ART

The Coming Up Roses gang quickly came to the attention of the DeCavalcante New Jersey crime family and Carmine Genovese invited them to his house. Over spaghetti and meatballs he hired them for a hit. They immediately drove out to the mark's home. When another gang member funked it, Kuklinski walked up coolly to the target as he sat in his car and blew his brains out. The gang members got $500 each.

Genovese then employed them as hijackers, but when two of his gang held up a card game run by a made man in the DeCavalcante family, Kuklinski quickly dealt with the situation. He shot them in the head before they knew what was happening.

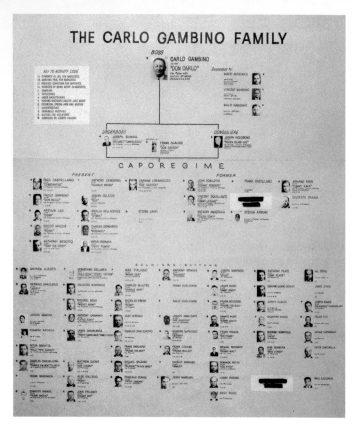

The Gambino family chart reveals the hierarchical structure of the Mafia. It was shown at a Senate crime inquiry in October 1963.

Now a lone wolf, he practised his art as an executioner by taking the ferry over to Manhattan and murdering down-and-outs and homosexuals on the run-down lower West Side. He killed with a knife, a gun, a rope and an ice-pick, figuring out the most efficient way of inducing death. He reckoned that he had killed more than fifty men there over the years.

SETTLING PERSONAL SCORES

In February 1956 he was playing pool in a bar in Hoboken when a truck driver called him a Polack. Kuklinski smashed a pool cue round his head and KOed another man with an eight ball. When he left, three men went after him. The truck driver attacked him with a length of pipe but Kuklinski shot him in the head and then killed the other two. He dumped their bodies down a sinkhole

in Bucks County, Pennsylvania, and pushed their car into the Hudson.

Kuklinski beat Linda, the woman he was living with, even when she was pregnant. But he never laid a finger on their children. Anyone who did was given a severe beating. Later Kuklinski killed a friend of his when he asked him to kill his wife and child, explaining: 'I don't kill women and I don't kill children. And anyone who does doesn't deserve to live.'

When Kuklinski discovered that Linda was having an affair, he broke down the door of the guilty couple's hotel bedroom, broke every bone in the man's body and then cut Linda's nipples off.

KILLER ON A SHORT FUSE

Carmine Genovese then commissioned Kuklinski for another hit. This time the mark was to suffer. Kuklinski tied the man to a tree and cut his fingers off one by one, then took a hatchet to his feet and legs. Finally he cut his head off to take back to Genovese, to show him he had done the job.

His reputation was soon so formidable that other Mafiosi steered clear of him. He always carried a knife and two guns, favouring a .38 Derringer. It was easy to conceal and lethal at close range – and Kuklinski liked to do his killing up close. He often used two different guns so that the police would think there was more than one gunman.

Genovese sent Kuklinski to Chicago to pick up some money. The mark kept telling Kuklinski that the money was coming. When he did eventually hand it over, Kuklinski killed him anyway for wasting his time.

A crooked police officer paid him to collect a suitcase from Los Angeles. Later he discovered that it contained a kilo of heroin and he had risked a long prison term. He killed the cop and buried him out in the middle of nowhere.

On another occasion, a man who aimed to welch on a $5,000 gambling debt had his brains splattered over the side of his car with a tyre lever. Another target was having sex with his girlfriend on board a boat. Not wanting to hurt the girl, Kuklinski waited half the night, then went and killed the mark, forgoing any torture as he was feeling in a good mood.

By the age of 24, Kuklinski was drinking heavily and getting into bar fights. When someone asked him to settle a difference outside, Kuklinski stabbed his opponent under the chin so hard that the blade penetrated his brain. Then a bouncer who kicked him out for being loud had his head beaten in with a hammer the next day.

BRIEF HIJACKING CAREER

Kuklinski briefly went straight and married Barbara Pedrici. To keep her in style he turned back to crime, stealing a truckload of jeans direct from a depot. While on his way to the buyer, he inadvertently cut up two guys in a red Chevrolet. After an altercation they came at him with a baseball bat. He shot them both in the head.

After Kuklinski had stolen a truck full of Casio watches, the buyer tried to renegotiate the price. He shot him in the head, along with the three men unloading the truck.

Another hijacked truck disappeared from a farm where he had left it. With a flare, he burned the farmer's foot off, then his testicles, until he finally admitted that a friend had taken it. He shot both of them in the head.

BOOTLEGGING PORN

Kuklinski then went to work at a film laboratory, where he also developed hardcore porn which he began to bootleg to the Gambino family. When a union official at the laboratory berated Kuklinski for hogging all the overtime, Kuklinski punched him. He went down hitting his head and another body disappeared into the Hudson.

Kuklinski was only arrested after he intervened when his brother Joe was being held hostage over a gambling debt. Loading his Derringers with dumdum bullets, Kuklinski fired them into the car driven by the men who were holding him, but had got rid of the guns by the time the police arrived. The men spent the night in the cells but were freed in the morning, after Kuklinski had arranged to get $3,000 to the judge.

The film laboratory where Kuklinski worked was just a block away from the famous Peppermint Lounge. One evening Kuklinski had trouble with a bouncer there. Three days later he arrived with a .22 revolver in a lunch sack, pulled out the gun, shot the bouncer in the head and walked away.

FULL-TIME CONTRACT KILLER

Now in the porn industry, Kuklinski ran across Roy DeMeo, who put the squeeze on him. Ambushed by DeMeo's crew of seasoned killers, Kuklinski could do nothing while DeMeo savagely pistol-whipped him. Later they agreed to go into the contract-killing business together. But first Kuklinski was put to the test. DeMeo gave him a .38 revolver and pointed out a man walking his dog. Kuklinski shot him in the back of the head.

For his first assignment, Kuklinski was given an address in Queens, a photograph of the mark and $20,000. He followed the mark, parked next to him and punctured his front tyre. When the man returned, Kuklinski offered to lend a hand, then pulled a gun and forced the man into the boot of his Cadillac. He drove him out to Pennsylvania, shot him in the head and dropped him down a sinkhole.

As he was not a made man, Kuklinski did not hang out with other mobsters and after a hit he went home to his family. They moved into a middle-class neighbourhood in Dumont, New Jersey, where Kuklinski was known as a good neighbour who gave extravagant poolside barbecues. Indoors, he still had bouts of uncontrollable rage and warned his children that if he killed their mother he would have to kill them too.

The next on the list was Paul Rothenberg, the lynchpin of the porn business. Kuklinski shot him down in a busy street while DeMeo looked on. While making his getaway, a man in a red Mustang cut him up so he shot him dead at the next stop sign.

TORTURE WAS A GAME

DeMeo then sent Kuklinski after a man in Florida who had raped a fellow Mafioso's daughter.

'Make him suffer,' he said.

Kuklinski abducted the man, tore his testicles off with his bare hands, removed his penis, stripped him, carved

> *I enjoy seeing the lights go out. I enjoy killing up close and personal. I always wanted the last image they had to be my face*

away his flesh, poured salt in the wounds, disembowelled him and then put him in a life jacket and floated him out to sea for the sharks to finish off.

On the way home through South Carolina, he was taunted by three rednecks. When they went for him with a club, he shot all three of them dead and drove off.

Back in Brooklyn, he handed DeMeo the victim's severed penis in a ziplock sandwich bag he had taken for the purpose. While the two men shared a plate of antipasto, DeMeo enjoyed Kuklinski's description of how the mark had met his end. By then Kuklinski had begun collecting torture ideas from movies and *Road Runner* cartoons, detailing them in a notebook. When a man in Los Angeles owed him $10,000, he went to his shop, handed him the pin from a grenade and dropped the grenade behind the counter. The blast threw people out of windows eight stories up.

A Sicilian Mafia boss did not like the man his daughter was seeing, so Kuklinski took the boyfriend out to the caves in Bucks County, wrapped in wet rawhide, with one strip around his testicles. He photographed his agony as the rawhide dried, then left him to be eaten – alive – by rats. Later he filmed these torture sessions and would watch them at night when everyone else had gone to bed. Even DeMeo could not bear to see them.

When a mark in LA proved elusive, Kuklinski rang his front doorbell, waited until he put his eye to the spyhole

MANHATTAN ★ ★ ★ SPORTS FINAL

COLOMBIA'S REIGN OF TERROR:

COCAINE KILLS

PART 4 OF WHY THE SMUGGLERS ARE WINNING — Starts on Page 7

DAILY◉NEWS

35¢   NEW YORK'S PICTURE NEWSPAPER®   Thursday, December 18, 1986

Nancy: They deceived Ron

Page 3

BURGER MURDER

N.J. man held in killings of 5 with gun & cyanide

Story on page 2

HASENFUS IS FREE

Nicaraguan President Daniel Ortega as he handed over gunrunner Eugene Hasenfus (left) to Sen. Christopher Dodd (right) in Managua yesterday. At far right is prisoner's wife, Sally. Hasenfus will arrive home today and may be summoned before congressional committees investigating the Contragate scandal. **Page 5**

The New York **Daily News** *front page dated 18 December 1986 headlines with the story of a Kuklinski murder where the perpetrator used his preferred method – cyanide.*

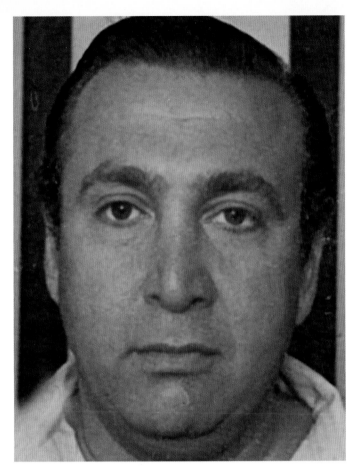

Gangster Roy DeMeo, for whom Kuklinski worked.

HIGH-PROFILE COMMISSIONS

When it was decided that the notorious Carmine 'Lilo' or 'the Cigar' Galante, then head of the Bonanno family, had to go, DeMeo suggested Kuklinski for the job. On 12 July 1979, Kuklinski had lunch in Joe and Mary's Italian restaurant in the Bushwick section of Brooklyn, where Galante liked to eat. He ordered a sandwich, so he would not leave any fingerprints.

The bodyguard who had fingered Galante got up from the table as two back-up gunmen came through the door. Kuklinski got to his feet, pulled out two guns and shot Galante and the other bodyguard. Then they walked to the car outside.

On the spur of the moment, Kuklinski shot a friend named George Malliband five times, then dumped the body in a back alley. It was known that Malliband had gone to meet Kuklinski that day.

After a meeting with John Gotti, 'Sammy the Bull' Gravano asked Kuklinski to kill a man named Paul Calabro, who cautiously took the back roads to his home in New Jersey. Kuklinski parked his van so Calabro would slow down and then shot him with both barrels of a shotgun. It was only the next day that Kuklinski learned that his victim was a decorated NYPD detective.

According to Kuklinski, John Gotti also had a special job for him. He went with John's brother, Gene Gotti, to abduct John Favara. Kuklinski said that he burnt Favara's genitals off with a flare and then stuffed them up his rectum, before Gotti cut him up.

Kuklinski then killed small-time crook Louis Masgay for one of his few friends, a fence named Phil Solimene who ran 'the store' in Paterson, New Jersey.

and then pulled the trigger. Contracted to kill a lieutenant in the Bonanno family, Kuklinski approached him in a disco with a syringe of cyanide. Everyone thought he had suffered a heart attack.

FAVOURED KILLING METHOD

Cyanide then became his favourite method of murder. He slipped it in drinks or sprinkled it on pizza or on a line of cocaine. He always used just enough to kill, but not enough to be detected.

Ex-Special Forces man Robert Pronge taught Kuklinski to use cyanide in a spray which was absorbed by the skin. He also taught him to keep the corpse in a freezer for a couple of months before dumping it, confusing the police about when the victim had died.

POLICE HAD HIM TAPED

Things began to unravel when a small-time burglar named Percy House told the police that he had been

On 12 July 1979 at a Brooklyn restaurant, New York police detectives cover the body of Carmine Galante, shot to death as he ate lunch. Police officials and witnesses said that four men pulled up in a car and opened fire with automatic weapons and shotguns.

part of a burglary gang run by 'Big Rich'. The gang had dispersed after Kuklinski had poisoned a member named Gary Smith. Then when Kuklinski killed another gang member named Danny Deppner, Percy House began to talk.

Checking out Kuklinski, the New Jersey police found he had a reputation for punching a hole in the windshield of the car of any driver that offended him.

Meanwhile, he killed Paul Hoffman, the chemist who supplied him with cyanide. Then he claimed to have killed DeMeo, pistol-whipping his corpse in revenge.

As more bodies that had connections with Kuklinski were found, Pat Kane, a single-minded New Jersey detective, contacted the NYPD's organized crime unit, and discovered that Kuklinski was linked to DeMeo, who was now dead.

The only exercise I ever got was carrying dead bodies

Although the police were on to him, the killings continued. He murdered a hitchhiker who gave him the finger and he killed a man in a secluded street just to try out a new mini-crossbow he had bought.

Solimene then came to the attention of the law and Kane persuaded him to let an undercover police officer named Dominick Polifrone, aka Provanzano, hang around 'the store'. But Kuklinski was on money-laundering business in Zurich, where he killed rivals with a cyanide spray and a knife. Back in New Jersey he killed the members of a ring of child abusers.

In 1985, Gotti and Gravano were planning to eliminate Paul Castellano. Kuklinski was called in to kill his bodyguard and driver Tommy Bilotti. When Castellano's car pulled up outside Sparks Steak House, two men approached wearing trench coats and Russian fur caps. Job done, Kuklinski and the other assassin then disappeared into the crowd.

With Kane on his trail, Kuklinski decided that the only way he could get rid of the nosy cop was with a cyanide spray and he asked Solimene if Provanzano could get him some of the poison. Polifrone telephoned Kuklinski and trapped him into admitting using cyanide in a spray, while the call was taped. They met at a service station where Kuklinski sold Polifrone a .22 revolver with a silencer. Polifrone then got Kuklinski to agree to a hit. He also talked of the murders of Smith, Deppner and Masgay. Everything was taped.

When Polifrone delivered the cyanide, Kuklinski spotted that it was not the real thing and took off. The police then stopped him driving away from his home.

Barbara Kuklinski

When Carmine Genovese was killed, Kuklinski was forced to take a regular job working for a trucking company. It was then that he met 18-year-old Italian Barbara Pedrici, a secretary with the firm. When he was sacked for talking to her, they started dating.

At 26, Kuklinski was considered too old for her. Barbara's family hired a private detective to check him out. When they learned about the type of man she had become involved with, they tried to break them up.

Barbara found him insanely possessive. When she said she wanted to go out with her friends, he stabbed her. He said that if she told her family, he would kill them all.

When she fell pregnant, she fled to her father in Miami. He went after her. They married. Barbara said: 'It was the worst day of my life.'

Back in New Jersey the violence continued. She lost three babies due to his beatings. When she was pregnant for a fourth time, she told him that if he ever raised a hand to their children, she would kill him. This he understood and accepted.

He did not pull the .25 automatic from under the seat of his car for fear that Barbara, who was in the car with him, might get hit. It took four men to wrestle him to the ground and handcuff him.

Kuklinski was formally charged with the murders of Deppner, Malliband, Masgay and Smith. When he discovered that Polifrone had been a plant, he knew he was sunk and mounted no defence. He was found guilty on all counts, but was spared the death sentence because there had been no eyewitnesses to his horrific crimes.

Already serving five life sentences, he pleaded guilty to the murder of Peter Calabro, earning himself another 30 years. Kuklinski was scheduled to testify against Gravano in the case when he died on 5 March 2006, aged 70.

THE SNAKE

Name: *Carmine Persico*

Aka: *Junior, the Snake, Immortal*

Born: *8 August 1933, Brooklyn, New York*

Gang affiliation: *Colombo*

Convictions: *murder, conspiracy to murder, hijacking, attempted bribery, extortion, loan-sharking, illegal gambling, parole violation, racketeering*

Carmine Persico is the last of the old-time New York Mafia bosses. He rose through the ranks from street thug to the head of the Colombo family, a position he held for forty years, though for much of that time he has been behind bars.

During the Depression, the Italian and Irish denizens of the Carroll Gardens and Red Hook neighbourhoods of Brooklyn, where Persico was brought up, scraped a living by working on the nearby waterfront or in factories. The Persico family was well off. His father was a stenographer for a prestigious Manhattan law firm and brought home a weekly pay packet even in the hardest of times.

The area was run by the Profaci crime family. The big bankrolls of the wiseguys drinking coffee and playing cards outside the local social or athletic clubs impressed the Persico brothers – Alphonse, Carmine and Theodore. At 16, Carmine dropped out of school and joined a street gang called the South Brooklyn Boys.

JOINING THE WISEGUYS

At 17, he was arrested for the fatal beating of another boy during a brawl in Prospect Park, his first felony. The charges were dropped, but they brought him to the attention of Profaci *capo* 'Frankie Shots' Abbatemarco, who employed the skinny, 5-foot-8-inch teenager as an enforcer. Persico then worked his way up through bookmaking and loan-sharking rings to burglaries and hijacking. By his mid-twenties, he was a made man.

American mobster Carmine Persico, age 17, after being arrested on charges of fatally beating another youth in Brooklyn, New York, 1951.

During the 1950s, Persico stacked up over a dozen arrests. His rap sheet ran the whole gamut of mob activity – running numbers, dice games, assault, harassing a police officer, burglary, loan-sharking, hijacking and possessing an unregistered firearm. But he never spent more than two weeks in jail. Profaci lawyers got felony charges reduced to misdemeanours, while plaintiffs and witnesses changed their minds or were out of town at the time of the trial. Fines were considered a business overhead.

LEAD-UP TO THE GALLO WAR

Persico was tight with the Gallo brothers – Larry, Albert and 'Crazy Joe'. When Albert Anastasia, the head of Murder, Inc., was gunned down while having a shave in the barber's shop of the Park Sheraton Hotel, Joey Gallo claimed it was the work of his 'barbershop quintet'. One of them was thought to be Carmine Persico.

When Frankie Shots was murdered, Persico and the Gallo brothers expected to inherit a large part of his Brooklyn rackets as a reward for icing Anastasia. Instead, Profaci's cronies were rewarded. The Gallo faction responded by kidnapping Profaci's brother-in-law and underboss Joe Magliocco, along with Joe Colombo and four other *capos*. The hostages were released after Profaci lifted the higher tribute payments he demanded from the Gallos. But Profaci quickly reneged on the deal and war broke out.

Recently retired mob boss Frank Costello convinced Persico that his loyalties lay with Profaci. On 20 August 1961, a police sergeant on a routine inspection of the Sahara Lounge, a bar in South Brooklyn, found Persico strangling Larry Gallo with a rope. Persico fled and Gallo refused to press charges. This perfidy earned Persico the soubriquet 'the Snake'.

Joseph Profaci, founder of the Colombo crime family, controlled prostitution, loan-sharking and narcotics trafficking in Brooklyn.

installing Colombo as boss of the Profaci crime family. Persico was promoted to *capo*. A rising star, he now wore well-tailored suits and his crew became one of the most profitable in the newly renamed Colombo family.

But a federal indictment for a 1959 hijacking was still hanging over him. A battery of expensive lawyers dragged the case out for 12 years. After five separate trials, he was convicted, thanks to the testimony of Mafia 'rat' Joe Valachi, and sentenced to 14 years. However, he was cleared of running a multimillion-dollar loan-sharking business when a key witness vanished before the trial started and another 12 failed to identify him in court.

In 1971, Joe Colombo was shot and paralyzed at an Italian-American civil rights rally. Although he was in prison, Persico took over the family with Tommy DiBella as acting boss.

Paroled in 1979, Persico was charged with attempting to bribe an agent of the IRS. Federal marshals looking for his brother Alphonse 'Allie Boy', then a fugitive, crashed a meeting Persico was holding in Brooklyn. He was immediately charged with violating his parole by associating with other known criminals. In a plea bargain, he went away for another five years.

SURROUNDED BY THE FBI

Released after just three years, he got wind that a RICO indictment was being prepared, alleging that he was the head of the Colombo family. He went into hiding in the house of Fred DeChristopher, whose wife Katherine was the sister of Andy 'Fat Man' Russo, Persico's cousin and a *capo* in the Colombo family. Terrified of Russo – who once, at dinner, held a fork to a man's eye and said 'Next time you f*** up, I'll push this fork right into your f*****g eye' – DeChristopher confessed all to the police. One morning soon after, DeChristopher's phone rang. A voice said: 'Can I speak to Mr Persico?' DeChristopher handed over the phone.

The Gallos struck back, peppering Persico's car with bullets. He was hit in the hand and arm, but he too obeyed the rule of *omertà*. While his supporters said that he had been hit in the face and had spat out the bullets, Persico himself referred to his wounds as paper cuts. In fact, he never regained the full use of his left hand.

In the 'Gallo War' that ensued, nine combatants were killed and three more disappeared, presumed dead.

A RISING STAR

When Profaci died of cancer in 1962, Magliocco took over, but the other dons intervened, forcing out Magliocco and

Persico's former associate and subsequent rival Victor Orena was indicted on charges of murder and racketeering in 1992.

Persico said: 'Who is this?'

The voice on the phone said: 'This is the FBI. We have the house surrounded. Come out with your hands up.'

Persico did.

At the ensuing 'Colombo trial', DeChristopher testified that, while preparing pasta with garlic and olive oil, his uninvited guest had boasted that he had run the Colombo family from jail and had stashed away enough money from his crimes to 'last ten lifetimes'. He also said 'I killed Anastasia' and bragged that he was one of Joey Gallo's 'barbershop quintet'. Persico went down for 39 years. His son Alphonse, 'Little Allie Boy', was sentenced to 12 years for being one of his father's lieutenants. In a separate trial, Persico was convicted of being a member of the Mafia Commission and was sentenced to another hundred years.

THIRD COLOMBO WAR

From jail Persico put out contracts on US Attorney Rudolph Giuliani, later mayor of New York, and other federal prosecutors. He also bribed prison guards for favours and arranged to have sex with a female attorney who visited him.

Running the family business from behind bars, Persico installed Victor 'Little Vic' Orena as acting boss until Little Allie Boy got out of jail. But Little Vic had ambitions of his own. After two years, he asked his *consigliere* Carmine Sessa to poll the *capos* to see who favoured him taking over permanently. Instead, Sessa informed Persico. On the evening of 20 June 1991, Orena returned to his home in Cedarhurst, Long Island, to find a five-man hit squad waiting outside. He sped away.

For three months, Orena's and Persico's factions

Gregory Scarpa before the Senate Investigations Subcommittee; he took the Fifth Amendment 60 times, refusing even to say where he was born. He was subpoenaed after two convicted men named him as a principal 'mob-fence'.

negotiated. Then bullets began to fly, in the third Colombo war. Orena was backed by Joe Profaci's son, Salvatore – aka 'Sally Pro' or 'Jersey Sal', as he ran the family's interests in New Jersey. He said that the Snake had gone crazy.

Persico's faction was led by Gregory 'the Grim Reaper' Scarpa, who was also an FBI informant. In 1964, when three civil rights workers disappeared in Mississippi, the Bureau employed Scarpa to find out what had happened to them. Scarpa kidnapped a Ku Klux Klan member, beat him up, shoved a gun barrel down his throat, and said: 'I'm going to blow your head off.' Realizing that Scarpa was serious, the klansman revealed that the bodies had been buried under an earth dam.

That December five Colombo mobsters were gunned down – one while hanging a Christmas wreath on his front door. Eighteen-year-old Matteo Speranza was murdered in the bagel shop where he worked by an Orena gunman who mistakenly thought he was a Persico supporter. Innocent civilians also died in the gunfire.

In an attempt to halt the war, Brooklyn District Attorney Charles J. Hymes subpoenaed 41 suspected Colombo family members before a grand jury. Only 28

This is the FBI. We have the house surrounded. Come out with your hands up

showed up and none of them would talk.

As the body count climbed, Scarpa contracted AIDS through a blood transfusion and lost an eye in an unrelated dispute over narcotics. The Persico faction then had to apologize to the Genovese family for accidentally killing 78-year-old Gaetano 'Tommy Scars' Amato, a retired soldier who had mistakenly been at an Orena social club when Persico gunmen paid a visit.

The FBI then subpoenaed Kenneth Geller, an accountant who worked for the Colombos. He had borrowed $1 million from their loan-sharking operation for a business deal that went sour and sought to escape his debt via the Federal Witness Protection Program. Geller delivered Orena, who was arrested at his mistress's home where agents found four loaded shotguns, two assault rifles and six handguns.

Orena was handed life imprisonment without the possibility of parole on the RICO charges of murder, conspiracy to murder and heavyweight loan-sharking. Sixty-eight *capos*, soldiers and Colombo associates also went down, including Orena's two sons.

Andy Russo, Persico's younger brother Theodore and enforcer Hugh McIntosh were also sentenced to long prison terms. Persico's elder brother Alphonse, 'Little Allie', who was already serving 25 years for extortion, died in jail. Finally Gregory Scarpa was arrested. His work for the FBI did not save him from a ten-year sentence for three murders and conspiracy to murder. He, too, died in jail. Nevertheless, the arrests ended the war and left Persico in charge.

In 2001, Little Allie Boy Persico went down for 13 years for loan-sharking. A life sentence for murder followed in 2007. Even so, Carmine Persico continued to run the Colombo family from the Federal Correctional Complex in Butner, North Carolina. The war he waged to maintain control cost 12 lives and led to some 70 wiseguys and their associates landing in jail.

Stool Pigeon

As a child, Joseph Valachi was known for his ability to build makeshift scooters out of wooden crates. This earned him the nickname 'Joe Cargo'. He had made the mistake of joining an Irish gang. This so displeased the Italian underworld that, while he was serving a prison sentence for theft, he was punished by a knife wound that ran under his heart and around to his back, requiring 38 stitches.

He got the message. After he was released, he joined the Mafia, starting as a driver. Then with the outbreak of the Castellammarese War, which pitted old-time Sicilian Mafia don 'Joe the Boss' Masseria against Salvatore Maranzano in 1930, he got the chance to advance his criminal career. He rented an apartment in Pelham Parkway, overlooking that of Steven Ferrigno, one of Masseria's lieutenants. It was from there that a team led by an assassin known as 'Buster from Chicago' shot and killed Ferrigno and Al Mineo, another of Masseria's lieutenants.

Although Joe the Boss escaped unscathed, Valachi became a made man for his participation in these killings. He then ran a numbers racket, an illegal 'horse room', slot machines and a loan-sharking operation.

During the Second World War, he made $200,000 from selling gasoline on the black market. In 1960, he was convicted for selling drugs and shared a cell in Atlanta Federal Penitentiary with Vito Genovese. Convinced that Genovese was going to have him killed, he beat another prisoner to death with a length of iron pipe. Then he broke the *omertà* and became the first man to admit to membership of the Cosa Nostra.

In 1963, he testified before Senator McClellan's committee which was investigating organized crime. His testimony on the organization and activities of the Mafia was so detailed that the McClellan hearings became known as the Valachi hearings.

Although the US Department of Justice banned the publication of Valachi's memoirs, they were used by journalist Peter Maas in his 1968 book *The Valachi Papers*. A movie based on the book, starring Charles Bronson, was made in 1972. After surviving a suicide attempt in 1966, Valachi died of a heart attack five years later at La Tuna Federal Correctional Institution in Texas.

THE LORD HIGH EXECUTIONER

Name: *Umberto Anastasio*

Aka: *Albert Anastasia, the Mad Hatter, the Lord High Executioner*

Born: *26 September 1902, Tropea, Calabria, Italy*

Died: *25 October 1957, Manhattan, New York*

Gang affiliation: *Mangano/Anastasia (later Gambino)*

Charges: *murder, conspiracy to murder, obstruction of justice, criminal association, carrying a concealed weapon, tax evasion*

The eldest son of a railroad worker, Umberto Anastasio began calling himself Albert Anastasia after his first arrest – 'to save the family from disgrace', his brother Anthony said. With three of his nine brothers he began working on board freighters after his father died in the First World War. They jumped ship in New York in 1919.

Working as a longshoreman, Anastasia was 19 when he was convicted of killing another worker on the Brooklyn waterfront. He spent 18 months in the death house in Sing Sing before winning a retrial. By then, four key witnesses had disappeared and he walked free. But in 1923 he was sent away for another two years for carrying a gun.

Anastasia used strong-arm tactics to take control of the International Longshoremen's Association. This brought him into contact with Giuseppe 'Joe the Boss' Masseria, the most powerful boss in Brooklyn. Masseria's top aides were Frank Costello and 'Lucky' Luciano, who worked with Vito Genovese, Meyer Lansky and 'Bugsy' Siegel.

OUT WITH THE OLD

During the Castellammarese War, Anastasia joined the other young turks to rid organized crime of the old-style 'Moustache Petes'. The war ended when Luciano lured Masseria out to lunch in a restaurant on Coney Island. When Luciano went to the bathroom, Anastasia, Genovese, Siegel and Joe Adonis came rushing in, guns blazing, killing Masseria.

When Luciano had first told him of the plan, Anastasia hugged him and said: 'Charlie, I have been waiting for this day for at least eight years. You're gonna be on top, if I have to kill everybody for you. With you there, that's the only way we can have any peace and make the real money.'

This was extraordinarily eloquent for Anastasia. Short and thickset, he was normally a man of few words and his Italian was scarcely better than his English. He had left school at 11.

MURDER, INCORPORATED

To prevent the infighting that had caused the Castellammarese War, the National Crime Syndicate, also known as the Commission, was set up. It was realized that this would need some 'muscle', so Murder, Incorporated was set up under the command of Louis 'Lepke' Buchalter and Anastasia, now underboss in the Mangano crime family. Over the next ten years, this gang of hitmen carried out some five hundred murders for 'business reasons'.

Its team of celebrated killers included Harry 'Pittsburgh Phil' Strauss, Frank 'the Dasher' Abbandando, 'Buggsy' Goldstein, Harry 'Happy' Maione – known for his permanent scowl – and Vito 'Chicken Head' Gurino, who practised by shooting the heads off chickens. Anastasia was also active. In 1932, he was indicted on charges of murdering a man with an ice-pick, but the case was dropped due to lack of witnesses. The following year, he was accused of murdering a man in a laundry, but again no witness could be found.

When Dutch Schultz found himself the target of special prosecutor Thomas E. Dewey, he demanded that Murder, Inc. hit Dewey. Anastasia came up with a plan. One of his men would walk up and down the street where Dewey lived, wheeling a pram. When there was no one about, he would pull out a sub-machine gun from under the blankets and cut Dewey down. However, Luciano,

Game over: gunned down in a Coney Island restaurant, Joe Masseria clutches the ace of spades – the death card.

Lansky, Costello and Adonis were against the idea as it was a direct violation of the rules the organization had been set up under. They were only to kill one another, not prosecutors, policemen, FBI agents, journalists or civilians, as it risked bringing down too much heat on them. Instead, Schultz was to be hit and Anastasia arranged it.

Murder, Inc. came to an end when one of its top lieutenants, Abe 'Kid Twist' Reles, was arrested for a number of murders and turned state's evidence. His testimony led to the arrest, trial and execution of lieutenants Louis Capone and Mendy Weiss, along with Pittsburgh Phil Strauss, Happy Maione, Dasher Abbandando, Buggsy Goldstein and Louis Buchalter, who was already in jail for narcotic trafficking and extortion.

Reles' testimony was also used to build a case against Anastasia. However, Reles fell to his death from the window of a hotel in Coney Island, where he was being held under ironclad police protection. This canary could sing, it was said, but he couldn't fly.

It burned and capsized in New York harbour. Luciano was then transferred from Dannemora, one of the toughest prisons in the system up on the Canadian border, to the more conducive Great Meadow Correctional Facility, closer to New York. In 1946, Thomas Dewey, now governor of New York, pardoned Luciano, who was released and deported back to Italy with a suitcase containing a million dollars supplied by Meyer Lansky.

HEAD OF THE FAMILY

Anastasia earned his United States citizenship by serving in the US Army as a technical sergeant training GI longshoremen in Pennsylvania. He remained underboss of the Mangano crime family, but frequently argued with the boss, Vincent Mangano. For 20 years he remained loyal. But in 1951 he formed a compact with Frank Costello, head of the Genovese family. Vincent Mangano then disappeared and has never been found. The same day, the body of his brother, Philip, was found shot to death in a swampy area near Sheepshead Bay. While he never admitted to the murders, Anastasia took

Meyer Lansky, known as the 'mob's accountant', developed an international gambling empire.

LUCIANO'S WAR EFFORT

Dewey managed to put Luciano away on pimping charges. In 1942, Anastasia developed an audacious plan to get Luciano out of jail. With the United States now on a war footing, there was a danger that the longshoremen could disrupt the war effort. Many of them were Italians and so were enemy aliens. However, Luciano could guarantee that there would be no problems on the waterfront through Anastasia and his brother, union boss Anthony 'Tough Tony' Anastasio.

But first Anastasia planned a little sabotage of his own. To draw attention to the danger America faced, he had his brother arrange a fire on the French liner SS *Normandie*, which had been seized by the United States government and was being converted into a troop ship.

> *You're gonna be on top, if I have to kill everybody for you*

over the family with the approval of the Commission.

After the war Anastasia bought into a dress factory and purchased a house overlooking the Hudson River in Fort Lee, New Jersey. He lived there with his wife and son behind a chain fence, guarded by a 'chauffeur' and watchdogs. He also bought a house in Italy for his aged mother and sister.

Both in front of the US Senate Special Committee

to Investigate Crime in 1951 and the State Crime Commission in 1952, Anastasia refused to say how he made a living, on the grounds of self-incrimination. He refused to tell them anything else either. In 1952, the federal government began deportation proceedings against him on the grounds that he had lied on his naturalization papers and had used fraud to obtain a 'certificate of arrival' from the Immigration and Naturalization Service. He had also said that he had never been arrested and had only used one name, Umberto Anastasio, neither of which was true. It was also alleged that for many years he had taken part in activities he knew to be prohibited by state and federal laws. But the courts ruled against the government and the case was dropped in 1956.

DODGING THE ASSASSINS

Several attempts had already been made on his life. When underboss Willie Moretti was killed in a restaurant in Cliffside Park, New Jersey, in October 1951, Anastasia was supposed to be with him. A few weeks later Anastasia was at a party in Newark, celebrating the acquittal of associate Benedicto Macri on a murder charge, when he had to flee out of the back door as gunmen came in through the front.

Meanwhile, Anastasia developed a greater passion for murder than ever. After watching a young Brooklyn salesman named Arnold Schuster on television, talking of his part in the arrest of America's most prolific bank robber Willie Sutton, Anastasia said: 'Hit the guy . . . I can't stand squealers.'

In March 1952 Schuster was shot outside his own home, twice in the groin and once in each eye. Anastasia had now violated the founding rule of Murder, Inc., first outlined by Bugsy Siegel: 'We only kill each other.'

In 1954 he was indicted on two counts of income tax evasion. The first trial ended with a hung jury. Before the retrial, the body of Vincent Macri, Benedicto Macri's brother, was found stuffed in the boot of a car in the Bronx. A few days later, Benedicto himself was found floating in the Passaic River. Another key witness was Charles Lee, a New Jersey plumbing contractor who had received $8,700 for work he had done on Anastasia's home. He and his wife went missing from their blood-splattered home in Miami, Florida. The government case now in tatters, Anastasia accepted a plea bargain and spent just one year in a federal penitentiary.

On 12 May 1936, Charles 'Lucky' Luciano (right) attempts to cover his face with a handkerchief while being transferred to a prison van. In 1998, Time *magazine characterized Luciano as one of the foremost criminal masterminds of the 20th century.*

VISIT TO BARBER'S CUT SHORT

At the time, Vito Genovese was trying to take over the Luciano family, but Anastasia supported his rival, Frank Costello. Normally Meyer Lansky would also have supported Costello, but Anastasia was trying to muscle in on his gambling operation in Cuba. Consequently, Anastasia had to go.

On the morning of 25 October 1957, Anastasia entered the barber's shop of the Park Sheraton Hotel. His bodyguard Anthony Coppola parked the car in the underground car park, then took a stroll. While Anastasia relaxed in the barber's chair, two masked men raced in. The shop's owner was told: 'Keep your mouth shut if you don't want your head blown off.'

Pushing the barber out of the way, they opened fire. The first volley brought Anastasia to his feet, but he did not turn towards his killers. Instead he lunged at their reflection in the mirror. Grabbing for the glass shelving in front of the mirror, he brought it crashing to the floor. There were two more shots – one in the back of the head.

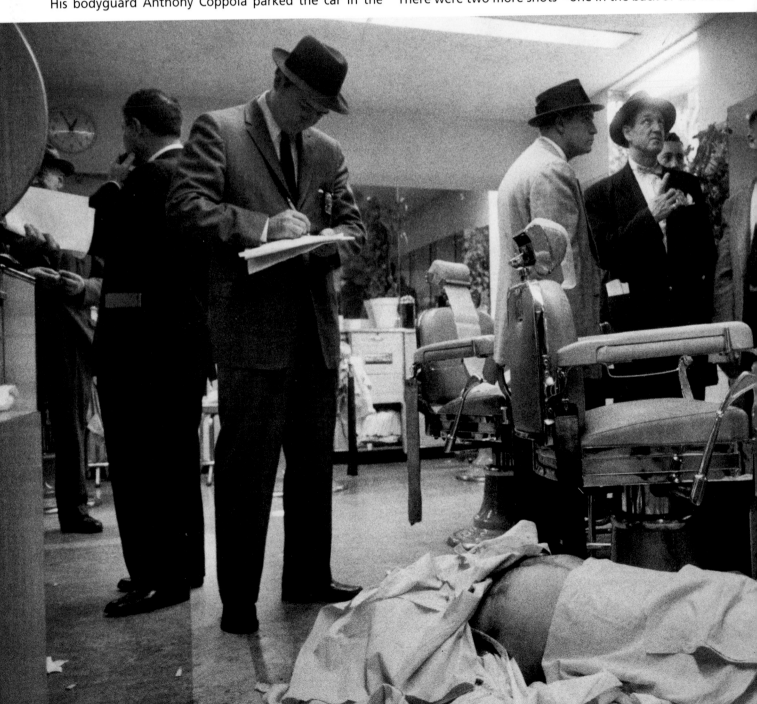

Anastasia was not afforded the lavish funeral normally given to a crime boss. There were just 12 mourners. No Mass was said for him, though his brother Salvatore, a Catholic priest, had visited the cemetery earlier and blessed the grave. Anastasia's obituaries in the newspapers said that he had been responsible for at least 63 murders.

Plain clothes detectives examine the barber shop of the Park Sheraton Hotel, New York, where the body of Albert Anastasia lies partially covered.

'Tough Tony'

Anthony 'Tough Tony' Anastasio was another of the four brothers who jumped ship in New York in 1919. While elder brother Albert pursued a career in homicide, Tony took control of Brooklyn Local 1814, a position he held for three decades. He also rose to become vice-president of the International Longshoremen's Association, running the Brooklyn waterfront with an iron fist. He only had to mention 'my brother Albert' to make his point.

And he was ever loyal. Once he confronted a reporter from the *New York World-Telegram and Sun* and asked: 'How come you keep writing all those bad things about my brother Albert? He ain't killed nobody in your family . . . yet.'

At Albert's behest, Tony organized the burning of the SS *Normandie*. He also prevented any further sabotage on the waterfront, stopped the enemy receiving details of sailings and helped US Navy Intelligence, who were operating on the dockside.

When Lucky Luciano was leaving for Italy, Tough Tony ensured that only top gangland figures were allowed aboard the *Laura Keene*, docked at Brooklyn's Bush Terminal, to bid him farewell. Reporters and other onlookers were held back by 50 longshoremen carrying menacing bailing hooks.

After Albert's murder in 1957, Tony's influence waned. However, Carlo Gambino, who succeeded Anastasia as head of the family, allowed him to retain control on the waterfront.

Fearing that Vito Genovese was out to kill him, Tony talked to the FBI. According to a memo dated August 1962, he told agents: 'I ate from the same table as Albert and came from the same womb but I know he killed many men and he deserved to die.'

In 1963 Tony Anastasio died of a heart attack in hospital. On the day of his funeral, all work was halted on the Brooklyn docks. Although he had a police record stretching back to 1925 with charges ranging from assault to murder, he had been cleared on every count.

BABY SHACKS

Name: Luigi Manocchio

Aka: Louis Manocchio, Baby Shacks, Baby Shanks, Baby Face, the Professor, the Old Man
----

Born: 23 June 1927, Providence, Rhode Island

Gang affiliation: Patriarca

Charges: murder, accessory to murder, conspiracy, theft, assault, extortion, possession of an illegal weapon, driving a stolen car, loan-sharking, illegal gambling
----

During his six decades as a career criminal, Luigi Manocchio worked his way up to being head of La Cosa Nostra in New England. Then, in the FBI's biggest ever one-day raid on organized crime, his empire came tumbling down.

Manocchio was first arrested in the 1940s, before he enlisted in the US Army in 1946. Being a soldier clearly did not suit him as he was discharged after just 14 months. Nevertheless, he still takes advantage of medical care at the VA Medical Center in Providence and he receives a military pension of $985 a month.

In 1948, he was arrested for robbery and was given a five-year suspended sentence. Four years later he was charged with two counts of assault and robbery, illegal possession of a firearm and driving a stolen car. His charge sheet already listed two of his nicknames – 'Baby Shanks' and 'Baby Face'. Everything but the weapons charge was dropped and he received another five-year suspended sentence. However, in 1955 he went to jail – for just 11 days.

In April 1968, bookmaker Rudolph 'Rudy' Marfeo was gunned down with his bodyguard Anthony Melei in Pannone's Market in Providence's Silver Lake district. Marfeo was found holding a .38 revolver, but he had been unable to loose off a single round. The hit had been on the orders of the gang boss at that time, Raymond L.S. Patriarca, who had told Marfeo to close down his rogue gambling operation.

ON THE RUN

The gunman, John 'Red' Kelley, joined the Federal Witness Protection Program, while Patriarca and several of his men were given ten-year sentences for conspiracy to murder. Manocchio was also arrested as an accessory, but was let out on bail. He then disappeared, spending ten years on the run in Europe, largely in France and Italy. It is thought that he returned to the United States several times, using a fake passport and wearing a disguise. It is said that on one occasion he dressed as a woman to escape arrest.

In July 1979, Manocchio returned to Rhode Island and gave himself up. He was convicted of being an accessory to murder and conspiracy, and was given two life sentences plus ten years. However, a key witness suffered from Alzheimer's disease and was found to have lied in a related case. Manocchio was released on bail. The ensuing court battle went all the way to the Supreme Court. Manocchio then cut a deal. He pleaded no contest to conspiracy and was sentenced to the two-and-a-half years he had already served.

Manocchio had earned himself something of a reputation among the Patriarca family, who referred to him simply as 'that guy'. While the headquarters of the New England family had moved to Boston when Francis 'Cadillac Frank' Salemme became boss, Manocchio remained in Providence as *capo* of a crew of thieves, loan-sharks and bookmakers.

In January 1995, a major push against organized crime nailed Salemme, Stephen 'the Rifleman' Flemmi and the Irish-American hoodlum James 'Whitey' Bulger. The power then shifted back to Rhode Island and Manocchio became boss.

THE SIMPLE LIFE

Manocchio is the very antithesis of the ham-fisted, cigar-chomping godfather. A small man, he is said to be a

Raymond L.S. Patriarca's crime family controlled racketeering operations in New England for more than three decades.

health nut. Rising early, he would jog around Providence golf course, stopping at a tree to do a series of pull-ups. He was also an accomplished skier.

'People watch mob movies and see these guys smoking cigars and living the good life. Louie Manocchio stayed in tremendous shape,' said Rhode Island State Police Colonel Brendan Doherty. 'He watched what he ate and would even recommend to his other mob associates they go on a diet.'

He did not dress flashily and maintained a low profile, like old-style Sicilian Mafia bosses. Until his arrest in 2011, he lived in a small apartment above a café in the Federal Hill section of central Providence and ran his crime family's operations from a Laundromat on nearby Altwells Avenue. He remained unmarried, but is thought to have three adult children.

He was also thought to have had a financial interest in several restaurants, though his name did not appear on any official document. But he had been seen chatting to customers – in Italian to those who understood it – and recommending wines.

After his plea bargain in 1988, he tried to steer clear of the law. But the police would keep tabs on him and make random visits to the Laundromat.

'He was always a gentleman to me and to law enforcement,' said Doherty. 'But he made his point known that we were on the other side of the fence, and "catch me if you can".'

However, in 1996 Manocchio was arrested at his elderly mother's home in Mount Pleasant, where he was installing appliances stolen from a store in Connecticut. He entered a no contest plea and was given three years' probation.

This was frustrating for Doherty as the police and the FBI knew Manocchio was a crime boss. He took care to avoid being seen around other gangsters, but in 2006 was photographed having dinner with underboss Carmen 'the Big Cheese' DiNunzio, who later got six years for bribery.

EXTORTION WITHOUT THREATS

Manocchio eventually stepped down as boss of the Patriarca family, and the power shifted back to Boston under Peter 'Chief Crazy Horse' Limone. This may have been because he was over 80, or because federal

Providence, Rhode Island

investigators were getting too close for comfort.

In 2008, two FBI agents approached him in a restaurant on Federal Hill after he had been handed an envelope by an employee of a local strip club. It was found to contain cash, protection money from the strip club's boss. Manocchio was with Thomas Iafrate, who worked as a bookkeeper at the Cadillac Lounge strip club. Iafrate was arrested along with Manocchio during the 2011 round-up that took 127 Mafia suspects into custody.

Manocchio pleaded guilty to extorting between $800,000 and $1.5 million in protection money from strip clubs including the Satin Doll and the Cadillac Lounge, but maintained he did not threaten anyone.

'By virtue of my position, I inherited the deeds of my

By virtue of my position, I inherited the deeds of my associates

associates,' said Manocchio. 'I don't want my family or any of my friends to believe I personally threatened anyone.'

However, Assistant US Attorney William J. Ferland said that after a strip club owner reduced his payment to the mob, Manocchio visited him and informed the owner he needed to pay $4,000 a month.

'It's his personal appearance. It is who he is and what he represents that constitutes a threat,' Ferland said. 'He fails to recognize that because of his position, these businesses were willing to pay. They weren't making charitable donations to La Cosa Nostra.'

He was sentenced to five-and-a-half years. The judge recommended that the 85-year-old serve his sentence in North Carolina or Florida, where the climate would be better for his health.

'I think you are going to make it through this prison sentence and come out on the other end,' the judge said.

There are conflicting stories about how Manocchio got his nicknames. One story told that he was called 'Baby Shanks' because he liked slim young women; another said the moniker referred to his short legs.

Mafia Takedown

Many Mafiosi were caught in the January 2011 'Mafia Takedown' – the FBI's largest mob round-up in history, which netted 127 alleged mobsters on charges ranging from loan-sharking to murder. As well as nabbing the top men in the New England Patriarca family, nearly the entire leadership of the Colombo family was taken into custody, and the Genovese, Gambino, Lucchese and Bonanno families were all affected.

Prize captive was Gambino *capo* Bartolomeo 'Bobby Glasses' Vernace, who had eluded justice for three decades. He was found guilty of murdering Richard Godkin and John D'Agnese, the hard-working owners of a Queens bar, in 1981, after a drink was accidentally spilt on the dress of mobster Frank Riccardi's girlfriend.

Philadelphia underboss Martin Angelina was sentenced to 57 months for a racketeering conspiracy. Family boss Joseph Ligambi and 12 other members of the Philadelphia Cosa Nostra were also arrested in the sweep.

Others cuffed included 73-year-old Benjamin 'the Claw' Castellazzo – aka 'the Fang', or just simply 'Benji' – who had been seen brandishing a gun to intimidate a target in East New York just weeks before his arrest. He was sentenced to 63 months for racketeering.

There was also Vincenzo 'Vinny Carwash' Frogiero, described by the FBI as a Gambino soldier. He got his nickname after running car washes for the mob in his younger days. Then there was Anthony 'Tony Bagels' Cavezza, who had a penchant for the humble bagel.

Also caught in the round-up were the colourfully named Jack 'Jack the Whack' Rizzocascio, Joseph 'Junior Lollipops' Carna, Frank 'Meatball' Bellantoni, Anthino 'Hootie' Russo and John 'Johnny Bandana' Brancaccio. Nicknames have been part of mob culture since Lupo the Wolf and Al 'Scarface' Capone. A threatening moniker is part of a mobster's profile. A lot of gangsters have names that are difficult to pronounce, so soubriquets are convenient. They also give them a degree of anonymity. But Mafiosi are often sensitive souls, so it is best not to address them by their nicknames – unless you want to sleep with the fishes.

SKINNY JOEY

Name: *Joseph Merlino*

Aka: *Skinny Joey, 'the John Gotti of Passyunk Avenue'*

Born: *16 March 1962, Philadelphia, Pennsylvania*

Gang affiliation: *Philadelphia crime family*

Charges: *extortion, bookmaking, drug trafficking, loan-sharking, aggravated assault, possession of a weapon for unlawful purposes, robbery, parole violation*

Joseph 'Skinny Joey' Merlino was born to the mob. His father Salvatore 'Chucky' Merlino rose to be underboss to Nicodemo 'Little Nicky' Scarfo, boss of the Philly mob after the death of Angelo Bruno (see page 62). Scarfo used Merlino Sr.'s bar to plan his takeover. Skinny Joey was also the nephew of Lawrence 'Yogi' Merlino, a Scarfo *capo* jailed for racketeering and murder. His sister was engaged to Scarfo hitman Salvatore 'Salvie' Testa. And he was at school with Michael 'Mikey Chang' and Joseph 'Joey Chang' Ciancaglini, who both became made men under Scarfo.

Joey Merlino used to hang out on the streets with Mikey Ciancaglini, Georgie Borgesi and Gaetano 'Tommy Horsehead' Scafidi, who was younger. 'They used to beat up girls, they used to rob people,' said Horsehead. 'They used to go into clubs and start fights.'

In August 1982, Joey Merlino and Horsehead's older brother Salvatore 'Tori' Scafidi stabbed two men at the Lido Restaurant in Atlantic City. Merlino was convicted of two counts of aggravated assault and one count of possessing a weapon for an unlawful purpose.

According to another friend: 'Joey Merlino was mob royalty and no way he wasn't going into the life . . . Joey was born to follow in his father's footsteps. How could he not? He was the son of an underboss. People on the street respected and feared him. Girls went crazy over him. There was always plenty of money and the best tables in expensive restaurants and no waiting on line at the nightclubs. Big time sports celebrities and movie stars wanted to hang with him.'

Keep your friends close: Nicky Scarfo Jr. (foreground) seen here as he is found not guilty of the murder of cement contractor Vincent Falcone on 2 October 1980. 'Thank God for an honest jury,' he declared. The friendship between Scarfo and Joey Merlino ended in 1984 and it is rumoured that Merlino was the masked gunman who attacked Scarfo in 1989.

FEUD WITH THE SCARFOS

In 1984, Joey and his father were barred from New Jersey casinos, and when Salvatore Merlino was stopped for drink-driving he attempted to bribe the police officer who pulled him over. Scarfo decided that the family did not need this heat and demoted Merlino Sr. for his drinking. This started a feud and Joey broke off his friendship with Nicky Jr., Scarfo's son. Scarfo Sr. was then convicted of conspiracy to commit extortion in 1987. RICO convictions the following year put him away for 45 years.

On Halloween night in 1989, Nicky Scarfo Jr. was shot and wounded eight times by a masked gunman inside a South Philadelphia restaurant. For years, police sources claimed that Joey Merlino was the masked gunman, but Merlino and his attorneys have always denied his involvement and no one has ever been charged with the attempted hit. Scarfo Jr. went to live in North Jersey and law enforcement sources claimed his father arranged for the Lucchese crime family to safeguard the younger Scarfo from further attempts on his life.

Convicted of robbing an armoured car in 1989, Merlino spent his time in jail plotting with Ralph Natale, a former friend of Angelo Bruno, to take over the

Philadelphia crime family – then headed by John Stanfa in Scarfo Sr.'s absence. According to Natale, Merlino admitted in prison that he had been the shooter in the 1989 Halloween night attempt on Nicky Jr.'s life.

Natale said he authorized and helped Merlino plan the gangland murders of Louis 'Louie Irish' DeLuca in 1990 and Felix Bocchino and James 'Jimmy Brooms' DiAddorio in 1992. He also said that other members of Merlino's organization, including defendants Steven Mazzone, George Borgesi and Martin Angelina, visited him at different times in prison to discuss those plans.

TAKING OVER THE FAMILY

At the time, neither Natale nor Merlino had been formally initiated into the mob, so they decided to initiate themselves.

'We'll make ourselves,' Merlino said. 'What's the difference if we have the button or not? We'll take over Philadelphia and kill John Stanfa.'

Merlino was formally initiated into the mob by Stanfa in 1992, while Natale was formally initiated by Merlino after being released from prison in 1994.

In 1993, war broke out between Stanfa and the Merlino faction. Merlino was injured in a drive-by

Joey was a hard-drinking, womanizing drug user who would strangle you . . .

shooting with a bullet in the buttocks, while Mikey Chang, who was with him, was killed. Stanfa's son Joseph was shot in the face in another drive-by shooting, this time in the rush hour on the Schuylkill Expressway.

Merlino went back to jail briefly for parole violation.

Then Stanfa was convicted of labour racketeering, extortion, loan-sharking, murder and conspiracy to commit murder and was sentenced to five consecutive life sentences. When Merlino got out of jail he took over the Philadelphia family, with Natale as titular boss because he had connections with the Genovese family in New York. But when Natale went back to jail for parole violation in 1998, Merlino took his place.

'LIKEABLE GUY' EVERYONE WANTS TO KILL

Merlino's men gave drug dealer Louis Turra a severe beating when he refused to pay the mob's 'street tax'. Louis was then found dead in a prison cell, having apparently hanged himself. In retaliation for the beating, his father Anthony Turra suggested throwing grenades into Merlino's house to kill him and his 'scumbag' girlfriend. But Turra then went on trial for racketeering and drugs offences. At 61, he was confined to a wheelchair. On the way to the court, he was shot dead outside his home by a gunman wearing a black ski mask.

Merlino himself survived at least ten assassination attempts – two of which were thwarted by the FBI – and there was a $500,000 contract out on him.

'I honestly don't know why so many people are seeking his demise,' said his lawyer, Joseph C. Santaguida of Philadelphia. 'He's really a likeable guy.'

CHARITY WORK

Despite his violent reputation, Merlino was also known for his charitable work.

'I thought he was a gentleman, always been a gentleman with me, and I understand he's done a lot of nice things for underprivileged children and, for that, I commend him,' said South Philadelphia resident Pat Bombito.

In 1999, Natale was facing fresh drugs charges

that would have put him away for life, so he decided to turn state's evidence. He admitted ordering three killings in a gang war for control of the Philly LCN's multimillion-dollar gambling and loan-sharking empire, a business enterprise that stretched from Philadelphia to Atlantic City.

Two years later, Merlino faced Natale in court while standing trial on 36 counts of racketeering, including murder, attempted murder, extortion, illegal gambling and trafficking in stolen property. Merlino also faced a drug-trafficking charge. He was acquitted of three counts of murder, two counts of attempted murder and the drug-dealing charges. Nevertheless he was still sentenced to 14 years for racketeering. 'Ain't bad,' he said. 'Better than the death penalty.'

NEIGHBOUR FROM HELL

After 12 years in jail, Merlino was released. He was no longer skinny, having spent much of his prison time in the gym bulking up. Although he went to live in a cul-de-sac in an upper-class area of Boca Raton, Florida, he showed little intention of settling down.

'We've had the police come several times,' said one neighbour. 'It's been very stressful living near them. There is always screaming and fighting.'

The neighbours said that what they found most disturbing were the banging noises in the middle of the night, as if furniture or equipment was being moved about.

'I'm not easily frightened,' another neighbour said, when told a convicted mobster lived a few doors away. 'I don't know who he is, but he does have a lot of visitors.'

Merlino appeared to work out of his home and named his wi-fi connection 'Pine Barrens'. This is a reference to the heavily forested area near Atlantic City, where Richard Kuklinski often disposed of bodies. It was the scene of one of the most famous episodes of *The Sopranos*.

In November 1995, Joey Merlino busies himself with charity work. Earlier that day, Merlino's rival, John Stanfa, had been convicted of murder, extortion, kidnapping and racketeering charges.

'I can tell you that I would not want to live next door to Joey Merlino,' said Stephen LaPenta, a retired Philadelphia police lieutenant who had worked undercover as a mob informant, and had infiltrated Merlino's inner circle. LaPenta, who was spending his retirement in Florida, still kept tabs on the flamboyant mobster.

'The Joey I know was a hard-drinking, womanizing, gambling drug user who would strangle you,' he said. 'If Joey sneezed, 20 people would hand him a handkerchief.'

EARLY RETIREMENT

Merlino was no stranger to Florida, having spent time there when working for Nicky Scarfo, who had a house in Fort Lauderdale. There was speculation that Merlino was still living 'the life'. While he was prohibited from associating with known felons, communication was easy enough in the digital age. He had been replaced as head of the Philly mob by Joseph 'Uncle Joe' Ligambi, though the law enforcement authorities speculated he was just a front for Merlino.

But Merlino insisted he is happy in Florida.

'It's beautiful down here,' he said. 'Great weather. No stress. People come here, they live to be a hundred.'

And he said he had no intention of returning to a life of crime.

'Too many rats,' he said. 'I want no part of that.'

In July 1999, Joey Merlino's mother and wife leave court in Philadelphia after an appeal by Merlino's lawyers asking for his release from prison pending his trial on drugs charges.

Brenda Colletti

In 1988, Brenda was a nude go-go dancer, supporting an unemployed husband. Then she met Philadelphia hitman Philip Colletti in the Dunkin' Donuts outlet she used on the way home from work. She had had a row with her husband and Colletti offered to take her for breakfast at Denny's.

Her husband walked in on them. Inflamed, he made a move to hit Brenda. Colletti put himself between them and said to him: 'If you touch her, I will kill you.'

Then he turned to Brenda and said: 'If you want to go with this piece of shit, then go. But if you're afraid of him, stay put, and I'll take care of you.'

Brenda said she was staying.

Colletti revealed that he was a small-time associate of the mob, who threatened gamblers owing money to loan-sharks. Brenda married Colletti in 1990 and they had a son.

By then, Colletti was working as a plumber, but he was laid off and began going out at night to meet acquaintances from his old neighbourhood. Brenda learned not to ask where he was going or what he was doing.

On his birthday he took her to a Bucks County restaurant where he introduced her to an older man with grey hair.

'Honey,' he said. 'This is John Stanfa.'

Later her husband explained that Stanfa was boss of the Philly mob. What he did not tell her was that Stanfa was at war with Skinny Joey Merlino at the time.

Because of his association with Stanfa, Colletti's life was in danger. He joined one of Stanfa's teams and roamed Philadelphia at night looking for Merlino's men. The crew would fetch up at Colletti's house and Brenda would feed them. Then they would start talking strategy.

'Here they were in my little

Brenda Colletti was working as a nude go-go dancer when she met her Mafia hitman husband.

house in the suburbs, trying to plan murder!' she said. 'They just wanted to find the other guys, pull out their guns, and start blasting.'

One night Colletti's friend Sal Brunetti suggested that they could hide under the front steps of a target's apartment building and then start shooting the second the front door opened. Brenda could not keep her mouth shut.

'What if the door opens and it's not him?' she said. 'You're gonna peg off an innocent person?'

She was told to 'shut the f*** up'.

One afternoon, Brenda got a call from Colletti, telling her to 'clean the house'. That meant hide all the arms and ammunition under a nearby woodpile. Then she heard on the radio that there had been a Mafia hit.

Colletti and John-John Veasey had been driving by Merlino's clubhouse when they had spotted Michael Ciancaglini and opened fire. Colletti's bullet had killed Ciancaglini, while Veasey's had wounded Merlino in the buttocks – making Colletti an instant hero among Stanfa's faction.

Fearing retribution, the Collettis began to sleep with guns under their mattress. They knew they would never be safe until Merlino was dead. Brenda volunteered to get dolled up, go to Merlino's favourite club and put cyanide in his drink.

Colletti was against the idea. Then there was a botched hit on Veasey and he contacted the US Attorney's office. 'He turned rat,' said Brenda. 'When that happened, Philip knew it was time for him to turn rat, too, or die. So he did, and we all went into hiding – even Philip's mom and dad.'

Once Stanfa's indictment was prepared, Colletti pleaded guilty to Ciancaglini's murder and other crimes. He got 12 years. Brenda was given three months probation. Eventually she divorced Colletti and settled in Nashville.

THE GENTLE DON

Name: *Angelo Annaloro*

Aka: *Angelo Bruno, the Gentle Don, the Docile Don*

Born: *21 May 1910, Villalba, Sicily*

Died: *21 March 1980, Philadelphia, Pennsylvania*

Gang affiliation: *Philadelphia crime family*

Charges: *reckless driving, bootlegging, firearms violations, operating an illicit alcohol still, illegal gambling, receiving stolen property*

Angelo Annaloro, the Gentle Don, was born in Villalba, Sicily, and went as an infant to the United States in 1911. His father, Michele, ran a grocery store in south Philadelphia. Young Angelo first came to the attention of the police when he turned in an extortionist who had tried to extract protection money from his father.

When he turned to crime, he changed his name, taking the maiden name of his paternal grandmother. Police records from the 1930s reveal that he gave his name as Angelo Bruno when he was arrested on illegal gambling and bootlegging charges. He was introduced to Philadelphia Mafia boss Salvatore Sabella by Michael Maggio, owner of the cheese factory in which he worked. In his thirties, Bruno became a made man.

FORCED RETIREMENT

When Sabella stepped down at the end of the Castellammarese War, Joseph 'Bruno' Dovi pushed aside John Avena to take over the family. He was succeeded by Joseph Ida. Under his regime, Bruno graduated from small-time bookmaker and gambler to major numbers writer and loan-shark, and was made *capo*. With underboss Marco Reginelli and *capo* Peter Casella, he ran the Greaser Gang whose bookmaking, gambling and loan-sharking operations turned over $50 million a year.

In 1953, a police raid uncovered 17,000 numbers slips

Annaloro maintained a successful gambling operation at the Plaza Hotel in Havana, Cuba.

By the mid-1960s, the Commission was headed by Carlo Gambino, who gave Bruno a seat. Bruno's alliance with Gambino enhanced his status and for two decades he maintained a 'Pax Mafia' in Philadelphia. As the Gentle Don kept violence to a minimum, this was largely tolerated by the authorities. Neil Welch, who later became Special Agent in charge of the FBI's Philadelphia office, said that for years the Bureau did not pursue Bruno with great vigour.

HITTING THE JACKPOT

Bruno maintained a front as a legitimate businessman, running the Atlas Extermination Company in Trenton, New Jersey and the Aluminum Products Sales Corporation in Hialeah, Florida, as well as retaining an interest in a casino at the Plaza Hotel in Havana, Cuba. Nevertheless, he chalked up further arrests for interstate tax conspiracy and filing false income tax returns.

When family member Nicky Scarfo stabbed a longshoreman over a seat in a restaurant, Bruno banished him to Atlantic City, then a depressed area. But in 1976 laws were passed to allow gambling there, in an attempt to revive the city. The rush was on to build casinos. Bruno had contacts in several steel companies in Pittsburgh and the Philly mob took a major hand in the construction work. They then moved in on all aspects of the gambling industry. Suddenly Scarfo was cock of the walk.

By then Bruno's hold on the family was weakening. He spent two years in jail for refusing to testify before a grand jury during an investigation into corruption in Atlantic City, involving a number of high-ranking officials. Instead of maintaining his monopoly, he allowed New York and New Jersey families to move in on the casinos in New Jersey. He also refused to become involved with the lucrative drugs trade. This caused resentment among the younger soldiers and *capos*.

in Bruno's headquarters. Convicted, he was fined and given two years' probation. But that did not stop him gambling and loan-sharking and he managed to escape several other prosecutions.

When Ida was deported to Italy, he had to choose between Bruno and Antonio 'Mr Miggs' Pollina as his successor. He chose Pollina. By then Bruno had his own loyal following, so Pollina sought to eliminate his rival. He gave the contract to underboss Ignazio 'Natz' Denaro. But Denaro told Bruno, who appealed to the Mafia Commission in New York. It was a dangerous move. If the Commission had found against him, he would have written his own death warrant. However, by asking for the Commission's arbitration, he had shown them respect.

Pollina had not asked permission to whack Bruno, who had already forged an alliance with Carlo Gambino. The Commission found in Bruno's favour, naming him the new boss of the Philadelphia mob and giving him permission to whack Pollina. Instead, Bruno forced him into retirement. This was typical of 'the Gentle Don', who sought to resolve disputes by diplomacy rather than murder.

Carlo Gambino

TIME TO GO

The 69-year-old Bruno was not in the best of health and faced indictments for racketeering. His *consigliere*, Anthony 'Tony Bananas' Caponigro, conspired with New York and New Jersey crime families to have Bruno wasted. He consulted Frank 'Funzi' Tieri, the acting boss of the Genovese family. Tieri gave his word that he would support Caponigro in front of the Commission.

On the evening of 21 March 1980, Bruno's driver, John Stanfa, took his boss home. As Stanfa pulled up outside Bruno's house at 934 Snyder Avenue, a man was waiting in the shadows. Stanfa pushed the button, lowering the passenger window next to Bruno. The man in the shadows moved swiftly towards it. He pulled a 12-bore shotgun from under his coat, put it to the back of Bruno's head and pulled the trigger. As Bruno slumped lifelessly, the gunman ran to a waiting car and sped off.

Stanfa was wounded when some pellets hit him in the arm. He was later charged with perjury relating to the testimony he had given in front of the grand jury investigating Bruno's shooting.

At Bruno's funeral, the cortege consisted of 17 limousines and 35 other cars. More than a thousand people filled the pavements outside the church.

Caponigro was summoned before the Commission, who said they had not given permission for the hit, nor had they even considered it. He turned to Tieri who, he said, had sanctioned the killing. Tieri denied it. As Caponigro had killed a Commission member without the Commission's consent, he was sentenced to death. On 18 April 1980, his body was found in the boot of a car in the South Bronx. He had suffered 14 bullet and knife wounds. His executioner was Joe 'Mad Dog' Sullivan, a Bronx enforcer.

POWER STRUGGLES

Over the next five years, 28 members or associates of the 60-strong Philadelphia family would die. After Caponigro's death, Bruno's underboss Philip 'Chicken Man' Testa took over the family with Scarfo as his *consigliere*. A year later, Testa was returning home when a remote-controlled bomb blew up his house. Testa's underboss Pete Casella claimed that he had been made boss at a meeting with Paul Castellano and Fat Tony Salerno. Scarfo discovered that he was lying. In exchange for allowing the Gambinos and the Genovese to operate in Atlantic City, Scarfo obtained their backing to become boss of the Philly mob and Casella went into retirement in Florida.

Then war broke out with Harry 'the Hunchback' Riccobene. War continued on and off for the next 20 years until the family was stabilized under Joseph 'Uncle Joe' Ligambi in 2001 – a far cry from the 20 years of profitable peace Angelo Bruno had given them.

A Philadelphia policeman checks the body of Angelo Bruno, who lies shot to death in his car.

John Stanfa

Born in 1940 in the tiny mountain village of Caccamo, some 30 miles from Palermo, Stanfa belonged to a Mafia family. Two of his brothers and one brother-in-law were members. After a car bomb in the Palermo suburb of Ciaculli killed seven policemen and military personnel, the authorities stamped down on the Mafia and Stanfa and his wife emigrated to the United States, settling in Philadelphia.

Stanfa had connections with Carlo Gambino and was seen hanging around known wiseguys. He was also a friend of Philadelphia crime boss Angelo Bruno, and became his personal driver. He was sitting next to Bruno when he was whacked. Indicted for perjury, Stanfa fled. After several months he came out of hiding and was sentenced to eight years.

When he got out in 1987, Scarfo was in jail

John Stanfa is taken from the federal magistrate's office in Hyattsville, Maryland, following the slaying of Angelo Bruno.

and the Philly mob was in tatters. Stanfa adopted a low profile, spending some time in Sicily. When he returned, Anthony Piccolo was acting boss, but the Gambinos and the Genovese backed Stanfa to take over, with Piccolo as his *consigliere*.

In many ways, Stanfa was as bad a boss as Scarfo. He increased the street tax that other thugs were required to pay La Cosa Nostra and sent old-time mobster Felix Bocchino out to collect it. When 73-year-old Bocchino was shot dead in his car, the press said it was the first Mafia hit in Philadelphia for seven years. It soon became clear that a bunch of young turks led by 'Skinny Joey' Merlino were responsible. Stanfa struck back with a botched hit on 'Mikey Chang' Ciancaglini. At that time, Merlino was in jail.

Stanfa beefed up his operation by bringing Rosario Bellocchi and Biagio Adornetto over from Sicily. He also patched it up with Merlino. Skinny Joey, Mikey Chang and Adornetto became made men. But Adornetto made a move on Stanfa's daughter, Sara. Bellocchi was sent after him with a shotgun and Adornetto fled.

Meanwhile, Merlino was making trouble. He liked to bet. When he won, he would collect his winnings; when he lost, he refused to pay up. Stanfa decided to go to war with him, but Merlino struck first. Stanfa's underboss, 'Joey Chang' Ciancaglini, was shot up in his social club. He survived, but was so badly injured that he was forced to retire.

Merlino made friends in jail with Ralph Natale, a serious rival to Stanfa. Stanfa ordered a hit on Merlino. He had a lucky escape when a bomb failed to detonate. Then, in August 1993, Merlino was injured while Mikey Chang was shot dead. Though Merlino was still alive, Stanfa thought he had taught him a lesson. He was wrong.

Three weeks later, Stanfa's car was stuck in traffic when a van pulled up alongside. The doors opened and shots came raining down on Stanfa's car. His son was hit in the face, but Stanfa and his driver managed to escape.

In retaliation, two top Merlino associates were hit. One vital member of the Merlino faction, Tommy 'Horsehead' Scafidi, then defected to Stanfa.

Merlino went back to jail for parole violation. Stanfa then discovered that they had an informer in their midst – the rat was caught by two bullets in his head. Nevertheless, on 17 March 1994, Stanfa and 23 of his men were indicted on racketeering charges that included murder, murder conspiracy, extortion, arson, kidnapping and obstruction of justice. Not only did the FBI have their informants inside the Philly mob, they had been bugging Stanfa since he had first taken over as boss. Bellocchi and others turned state's evidence to escape long prison sentences. For Stanfa, there was no one left he could inform on. In November 1995, he was sentenced to five consecutive life sentences.

THE LAST DON

Name: *Joseph Charles Massino*

Aka: *the Ear, Big Joey*

Born: *10 January 1943, Queens, New York*

Gang affiliation: *Bonanno*

Charges: *murder, labour racketeering, extortion, arson, illegal gambling, loan-sharking, money laundering*

Born to Italian-American parents, Joey Massino was brought up in Maspeth, a working-class area of Queens, New York. He dropped out of high school before graduating and went instead into the lunch-wagon business, selling snacks and soft drinks at factories and construction sites. But his trucks were a cover for illegal gambling, loan-sharking and selling stolen goods. He soon became known to the police as a rookie wiseguy.

A burly 5 feet 9 inches, he ate too many of his own sandwiches and doughnuts. His weight ballooned to 250 pounds and he became known as 'Big Joey'. In 1960, he married Josephine Vitale and his brother-in-law Salvatore 'Good Looking Sal' Vitale became his right-hand man.

A teenage friend was the nephew of Philip 'Rusty' Rastelli, a *capo* in the Bonanno family who was based in Maspeth. Rastelli was the kingpin of a hijacking operation that pulled off five or six road robberies every week in the New York area. Maintaining his thriving 'roach coach' business, Massino and his team successfully branched out into hijacking. As a protégé of Rastelli, Massino was 'made' in the Bonanno crime family.

SUPPLY AND DEMAND

Most heists took place with the gang blocking the truck and a team member jumping on to the running board and sticking a gun in the driver's face. Massino used a different method. Thanks to his loan-sharking business, he could organize 'give ups', when a teamster, or truck driver, could not afford to pay. That is, the truck driver handed over the goods without fuss. Using this method, he is thought to have got away with $100,000 worth of

The Manhattan skyline from Queens: Joe Massino, John Gotti and Charlie Carneglia all operated out of this borough.

coffee, $500,000 worth of clothing on its way to Saks Fifth Avenue and $2 million worth of Kodak film.

The key to his success was organizing 'drops' – empty warehouses or lots where the contraband could quickly be off-loaded on to smaller trucks for delivery to fences or pre-arranged clients. Massino's contacts were so good that he organized drops and fences for other hijackers. Soon he was running an underground clearing house for stolen goods – everything from lobsters to air-conditioners. This brought him into contact with another hijacker, John Gotti. They became neighbours when Massino moved his family out to Howard Beach.

However, the FBI were on his trail. On one occasion, they thought they had him cornered in a warehouse full of stolen goods. But as they rushed in at the front door, Massino vanished out the back, down a pre-planned escape route. Another time it was discovered that he was off-loading expensive suits via a rope line from the warehouse to a clothes shop, when a customer dropped in for a cut-price purchase.

'He was smart and feared and nobody would give him up,' said one agent.

FBI agent Patrick F. Colgan spotted a hijacked truck outside a diner in Maspeth one night. He tried to follow it, only to be blocked by a car that then sped off. When the car caught up with the truck, Massino jumped out of it and then climbed up on to the truck's running board. He had a word with the truck driver, then leapt back into the car and took off.

Colgan assumed that Massino had told the driver to dump the rig and then try to escape. He managed to catch up with the truck before that happened and was

Joseph Massino appeared as a defendant in the Rastelli-Bonanno family trial, September 1986.

holding the driver, Ray Wean, at gunpoint when Massino turned up and asked what was going on. Colgan told Massino that he was under arrest, but Massino said that he needed to relieve himself first. He then drove off. Two days later, Massino gave himself up. He stood trial on his first felony charge for theft from an interstate shipment. While Wean was convicted and spent a year in prison, Massino's attorney argued that his client had innocently stopped to find out if Wean, a casual acquaintance, was having trouble. He was acquitted.

FAILED TAKEOVER BID

While Carmine Galante was in jail in the 1970s, Rastelli took over as boss of the Bonanno family. But when Galante was paroled, Rastelli was in jail, and he took over again. Nevertheless, Massino remained loyal to Rastelli and visited him in prison. This enraged Galante and Massino feared that Galante might whack him. But before this could happen the Commission gave Rastelli permission to take out Galante. Massino was outside the restaurant as back-up when the hit was made.

Massino had previous experience of murder. He and John Gotti had killed and dismembered Paul Castellano's daughter's boyfriend, Vito Borelli, after he said that Castellano looked like Frank Perdue, the well-known purveyor of poultry. Joseph 'Do Do' Pastore, a cigarette smuggler and loan-shark, was also whacked by Massino, just because Massino owed him $9,000.

With Galante dead, Rastelli became boss of the Bonanno family again. But he was in jail, so he made the *capo* Salvatore 'Sally Fruits' Ferrugia acting boss. Massino was also promoted to *capo*, but the Bonanno soldiers knew that Massino had the direct line to Rastelli.

In May 1981, Massino heard from a Colombo soldier

that three Bonanno *capos* – Philip 'Phil Lucky' Giaccone, Alphonse 'Sonny Red' Indelicato and Dominick 'Big Trin' Trinchera – aimed to take over. Massino consulted Paul Castellano and Carmine Persico, who told him to 'do what you have to do'.

The three renegade *capos* were invited to an 'administration meeting' in a Brooklyn social club run by the Gambinos. Weapons were traditionally not carried at these events, so it was all the more of a surprise to them when they were gunned down by masked men.

LEND ME YOUR EARS

At the time, undercover FBI agent Joseph Pistone had penetrated the Bonanno family under the alias Donnie Brasco. By then he had collected enough evidence to put the key players away for a long time. When Massino discovered this, he ordered a hit on Dominick 'Sonny Black' Napolitano, who had nominated Pistone.

When the first wave of indictments was handed down in the wake of the Donnie Brasco investigation, Massino's name was not on the list. He had been wary of Pistone from the beginning and had always been cautious about government surveillance. He would not even let people refer to him by name. Instead, when they spoke about him they were to tug their ears – hence his nickname.

Nevertheless, he figured that it would only be a matter of time before he was arrested, so he went into hiding. He still managed to run the family during this period – first from the Hamptons, then from the Pocono Mountains in Pennsylvania.

DODGING THE MURDER RAPS

In July 1982, Massino was indicted for conspiracy to murder the three *capos*. Two years later, in 1984, Rastelli was released from prison. He and Massino then arranged the murder of Cesare Bonventre, a Bonanno soldier. Their complaint was that he had not helped Massino while he was on the run. By this time, most members of the Bonanno family considered Massino the boss, though Rastelli remained titular head.

After consulting a lawyer, Massino handed himself in on 7 July 1984, confident that he could beat the rap. He was released on $350,000 bail. But more indictments followed. He was charged with conspiracy to murder Do Do Pastore and labour racketeering. He and Rastelli had controlled Teamsters Local 814, where they ran a scam in moving and storage. Found guilty, he was sentenced to ten years.

Although Wean and Pistone testified against him, Massino was cleared of the murder charges. He was found guilty of a 1975 hijacking, but it fell outside the RICO act's five-year statute of limitations, so he was cleared of that as well.

LIFE FOR 'THE LAST DON'

When Rastelli died in 1991, Massino became boss of the Bonanno family. He was released the following year, at a time when other crime bosses such as John Gotti, head of the Gambino family, were going to jail. So the newspapers started calling him 'the Last Don'. In proper godfather style, he held court in the CasaBlanca restaurant in Maspeth. But then, to save himself, his underboss Salvatore Vitale agreed to testify against him. Others followed.

On 9 January 2003, the FBI picked up Massino at his home in Howard Beach, Brooklyn, to face 19 federal charges. More charges soon followed. FBI assistant director Pasquale J. D'Amuro said: 'Massino is the most powerful mobster in the country.'

He went on trial the following year, facing charges related to seven murders, loan-sharking, arson, gambling, money laundering and extortion. The trial lasted for nine weeks and featured more than 70 witnesses, including Massino's brother-in-law and

Mobster Louis Tuzzio lies slumped in the driver's seat of his Chevrolet Camaro with a bullet in the back of the head. He was murdered by the Bonanno family on 3 January 1990.

six other members of the Bonanno family. He was convicted on 11 counts, including the murders of the three *capos* and Dominick Napolitano.

The FBI was not finished with him yet. Massino was to be tried for the 1999 murder of a Bonanno assassin named Gerlando 'George from Canada' Sciascia, who had been in on the murder of the three *capos*. This time the US Attorney General John Ashcroft sought the death penalty.

When the authorities also made it clear that they planned to strip him of all his assets, leaving his family homeless and penniless, Massino reconsidered his position and began to co-operate, giving evidence against Vincent 'Vinny Gorgeous' Basciano, who had become acting head of the Bonanno family.

In 2005, Massino pleaded guilty to the murder of Sciascia and received a life sentence on top of the life sentence he had received for his previous convictions. However, his forfeiture was lowered from $10 million to $9 million.

Basciano was also sentenced to life imprisonment and other top players ended up in jail. The Bonanno family never recovered from the investigative work of Donnie Brasco.

Donnie Brasco

Undercover FBI agent Joseph Pistone spent six years infiltrating the Bonanno crime family. Brought up in Paterson, New Jersey, he joined the FBI in 1969. In 1974, he was transferred to New York to work on the truck hijacking squad. With a Sicilian heritage and fluent Italian, as well as the ability to drive an 18-wheel truck, he was perfectly positioned to infiltrate the hijacking gangs. Having been raised in a working-class area as the son of a bar owner, he also knew 'the life'.

The FBI erased all record of Pistone's former life and constructed a new identity for him as Donald 'Donnie the Jeweler' Brasco, a small-time burglar. This gave him a non-violent reputation, so he would not be asked to hurt people. But he had to learn the street value of gems, and how to pick locks and dismantle alarms.

His undercover work started off as a six-month assignment and kept getting extended as he earned the trust of Dominick 'Sonny Black' Napolitano and Benjamin 'Lefty Guns' Ruggiero, who told him: 'As a wiseguy you can lie, you can cheat, you can steal, you can kill people – legitimately. You can do any goddamn thing you want and nobody can say anything about it. Who wouldn't want to be a wiseguy?'

In the 1970s, the US and Italian mafias had set out to control the world heroin trade, but there was friction between the American wiseguys and the Sicilian 'zips' who came to the States. Pistone exploited this rift.

Pistone nearly lost his life when Bonanno soldier Tony Mirra accused him of stealing $250,000 from the crime family. Pistone had three sit-down meetings with Mirra and representatives of the family and was eventually found to be innocent, though Mirra was

Johnny Depp and Al Pacino in **Donnie Brasco**

later whacked for introducing Pistone to the family.

Then it came time for him to become a made man. For this he would have to kill someone. Fortunately the guy he was supposed to whack had disappeared.

In 1981, when Massino took out the three *capos*, the FBI decided it was too dangerous for Pistone to continue. When he was pulled out, top mobsters were offering $500,000 for a hit on Pistone or his wife and children, before he could testify. He and his relatives were relocated and given 24-hour protection.

Meanwhile two FBI agents paid a night-time call on Fat Tony Salerno, boss of the Genovese family and member of the Commission. He was told that if Pistone or his relatives were harmed or threatened, there would be massive retaliation.

'Get the word out, Tony,' he was told. 'Leave Pistone alone.'

Salerno replied: 'We don't hurt cops, we don't hurt agents. Hey, you boys have a job to do, you got my guarantee.'

For his undercover work, Pistone was given a $500 bonus by the FBI. He retired in 1996, but continued to live under an assumed name for his own protection.

'It's not the wiseguys I'm most worried about,' he said. 'They respect me. They know I just did my job. I never entrapped anyone, never got them to do something they wouldn't have done anyway. But there's always the chance of running into someone who thinks he's a cowboy, you know, someone who doesn't like what you did.'

He wrote a book about his undercover work called *Donnie Brasco: My Undercover Life in the Mafia*, which was published in 1988. This was made into the 1997 movie *Donnie Brasco*, starring Johnny Depp as Pistone and Al Pacino as Ruggiero.

THE LOST DON

Name: *Giuseppe Lombardi*

Aka: *Joseph Patrick Lombardo, JL, Joey the Clown, Joe Padula, Lumpy, Lumbo, Emmett Kelly, Pagliacci*

Born: *1 January 1929, Chicago, Illinois*

Gang affiliation: *the Chicago Outfit*

Charges: *labour racketeering, fraud, extortion, bribery, loan-sharking, arson, kidnapping, resisting arrest*

Born to Italian immigrants, Lombardi dropped out of school. He committed his first theft at 18 so that his mother could get an operation. Known for his humour – earning him the nickname 'the Clown' or 'Pagliacci' – he changed the last letter of his name to an 'o' when he joined the Outfit. On the streets he was known as 'Lumpy', because he was so good at giving people lumps on their heads.

Lombardo made his way up the crime ladder as a jewel thief, a juice loan collector and a hitman. Quickly rising to become *capo* of the Grand Avenue crew on Chicago's North Side, he had 30 soldiers under him and ran the same streets in the Grand-

Ogden area as Tony 'the Ant' Spilotro and Tony Accardo's Circus Café Gang.

YOUNG ENTREPRENEUR

At the age of 25, Lombardo owned a construction company. Over the years, he also owned a trucking company, was said to be a worker for a hot-dog stand manufacturer, and had hidden holdings in restaurants and real estate. Meanwhile he was racking up arrests for burglary and loitering, though in each case he avoided conviction.

In 1963, his name was linked with John 'No Nose' DiFronzo, later boss of the Chicago Outfit, in a West

*In October 1957, members of the Teamsters labour union (with a jackass mascot)
root for the election of Jimmy Hoffa, an activist with mob connections. By the 1950s,
organized criminals had infiltrated the Teamsters and corruption had become endemic.*

Side loan-sharking ring. Lombardo and five others were accused of abducting a factory worker who owed $2,000, tying him to a beam in a basement and beating him unconscious. In court the man could not identify his assailants and Lombardo walked free – his 11th acquittal following 11 arrests.

Lombardo's activities included loan-sharking, illegal gambling and selling pornography. He even ran a ring dealing in stolen furs that operated at four Midwestern airports, including O'Hare. His men wore overalls so that they looked like airport workers.

Identified as a rising star, Lombardo was one of a thousand guests invited to a party honouring West Side overlord Fiore 'Fifi' Buccieri at the Edgewater Beach Hotel. This was 'the largest assemblage of mobsters ever staged in Chicago', the police said. They were entertained by crooner Vic Damone and a 20-piece band.

While the Chicago mob moved into Las Vegas, Lombardo stayed at home in the Windy City making so much money that he was a regular reader of the *Wall Street Journal*. He oversaw Tony Spilotro and Frank 'Lefty' Rosenthal in Las Vegas and liaised with Allen Dorfman,

In 2013, a detective gathers up crime scene tape during the search in a field near Detroit for the remains of former Teamsters union president Jimmy Hoffa, who went missing in 1975. The police were acting on a tip from Tony Zerilli, a former mobster.

whose father had introduced Jimmy Hoffa to the mob. Dorfman ran the Teamsters' pension fund, which was used to buy new casinos.

DIPPING INTO THE PENSION FUND

Meanwhile Lombardo was keeping his hand in as a hitman. In 1973, two men carrying shotguns walked into Rose's Sandwich Shop on Grand Avenue, lined the customers up against the wall and picked out disgraced police officer Richard Cain. He was Sam Giancana's bag man and did other work for the mob, while acting as an informant for the FBI. The gunmen put their shotguns under Cain's chin and blew his head off. One of the trigger men was said to be Lombardo.

In 1974, Lombardo, Spilotro and Dorfman were charged with defrauding the Teamsters' pension fund of $1.4 million. The money was being siphoned through the American Pail Company, a front organization run, some say unwittingly, by 29-year-old Daniel Seifert. Tony Accardo, who was then running the Chicago Outfit, told Lombardo to take Seifert out. He was shot dead by four masked gunmen in front of his wife and child. Again Lombardo was said to be one of the trigger men. Without Seifert, the fraud case fell apart and the defendants were acquitted.

According to FBI informants, Lombardo had authorized the killing of Indiana oilman Ray Ryan, a millionaire, when he stopped paying off one of Lombardo's associates. Another informant asked Lombardo's permission to whack a man who had damaged his disco in Schiller Park.

'Break the guy's arms, legs and head instead,' Lombardo replied. 'But if the problem occurs again, do whatever you have to do.'

SHARING A JOKE

Lombardo and James 'Legs' D'Antonio were sitting in a car when the police went to raid an illegal gambling den. They sped off. Officers pursued them. After a six-minute high-speed chase, they stopped the car and tried to walk innocently away, while Lombardo threw some notebooks over a fence. The police arrested the two men and recovered the notebooks. They contained the licence plate numbers of the cars that were chasing them and a number of off-colour jokes. Lombardo was, after all, 'The Clown'.

Six thousand dollars was found in his pocket; another $6,000 in his shoes. In court, explaining their frantic flight, Lombardo said: 'I had $12,000 on me. Those guys might have been robbers or killers.' He was found guilty of resisting arrest.

CASH FOR FAVOURS

The FBI put a phone tap on all the lines from Dorfman's office, seeking to prove the Outfit's ownership of several casinos in Las Vegas. Instead they listened in on a bribery scheme. The Teamsters would sell a plot next to the Las Vegas Hilton, to US Senator Howard Cannon of Nevada, at a knock-down price. In return, he would kill a bill deregulating the trucking business.

Lombardo, Dorfman, Teamsters' president Roy Williams and others were indicted. As the trial progressed, jurors were approached by menacing strangers. Nevertheless, they found the defendants guilty of 11 counts of bribery, fraud and conspiracy. While out on bail awaiting sentence, Dorfman was killed by a shotgun blast. Apparently the mob thought he was too soft to serve time and might inform on them.

Lombardo told the judge: 'I never ordered a killing. I never OK'ed a killing. I never killed a man in my life. I never ordered or OK'ed any bombing or arson in my life.'

The judge praised his eloquence and sentenced him to 15 years. From behind bars, Lombardo continued to protest his innocence.

'I have no faith in the system,' he said.

Soon after, Lombardo was convicted of skimming almost $2 million from Las Vegas casinos and was sentenced to another 16 years, running concurrently. Tony Spilotro was also facing trial. He and his brother Michael were found in a shallow grave in Indiana. The man who was supposed to have disposed of the bodies, John Fecarotta, was then killed for his incompetence.

ADVERTISING HIS INNOCENCE

Lombardo was paroled in 1992, only to make his most public joke yet. He put a small ad in a number of Chicago papers that said: 'I never took a secret oath with guns and daggers, pricked my finger, drew blood or burned paper to join a criminal organization. If anyone hears my name used in connection with any criminal activity please notify the FBI, local police and my parole officer, Ron Kumke.'

Nevertheless, back in the old neighbourhood, Lombardo still played the big-time mob boss. His pal Chris 'the Nose' Spina lost his job as a foreman at the First Ward sanitation yard in 1993, when the city alleged he was

> *Break the guy's arms, legs and head . . . do whatever you have to do*

spending his time chauffeuring Lombardo around town while he was clocked in at work. In 1997, a Cook County judge reinstated Spina – with back pay.

'He's seen as a spy of the Clown,' the *Chicago Tribune* reported.

After several years, DNA evidence tied the death of Big John Fecarotta to mob enforcer Nick Calabrese, who was already serving time in Michigan. Confronted with this, Calabrese flipped and told the FBI the inner workings of the Outfit. He gave details on 18 gruesome gangland murders and the FBI started Operation Family Secrets.

THE MISSING CLOWN

In 2003, the FBI approached Lombardo in the masonry shop where he worked and took a saliva swab and a hair sample. They were hoping to match the DNA to a strand of hair found in a ski mask left in the getaway car used in the Seifert murder. Agents also warned Lombardo that his life was in danger.

Lombardo was indicted for his role in at least one murder, as well as for illegal gambling and loan-sharking. But before the arrest warrant was issued, he disappeared. While 14 other defendants appeared in court, everyone wondered where the 'Lost Don' was.

The *Chicago Tribune* put a picture of a cigar-chomping man on the front page of their Metro section

Lombardo, Frank Calabrese Sr. and James Marcello in court in 2007, facing charges stemming from Operation Family Secrets.

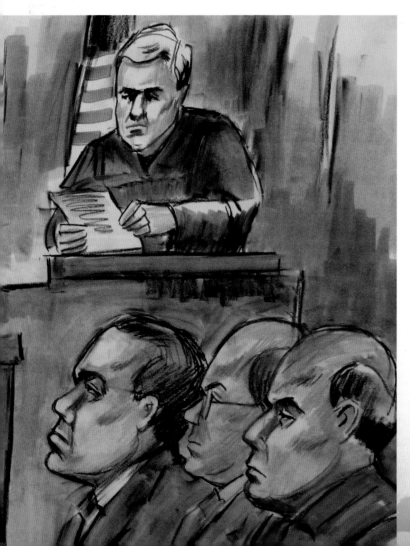

under the headline: 'Have you seen this "Clown"?' Only it wasn't Lombardo, just someone who looked like him.

The Clown himself then began to write to the judge, claiming he was innocent and spelling out terms for his surrender. He signed himself: 'Joe Lombardo, A Innocent Man.' In the letter, he made it clear that he was not going to flip. This was a message to the mobsters who might be on his tail.

JOKE OVER

A $20,000 reward was put on Lombardo's head and after nine months he was captured following a visit to his dentist – who just happened to be Tony Spilotro's brother, Patrick.

Lombardo pleaded not guilty. In court it was revealed that he was suffering from atherosclerosis, but had not seen a doctor.

'I was unavailable,' he explained.

Unusually, Lombardo took the stand in his own defence, claiming that he was in a police station reporting the loss of his wallet at the time of Seifert's slaying. But employees of an electronics store identified Lombardo as the man who had bought a police scanner used during the murder, and Lombardo's fingerprint was found on the title application of the car used.

He was found guilty of murder, racketeering, extortion and loan-sharking. At his sentencing, he complained: 'I was not given a fair trial and now I suppose the court is going to sentence me to life in prison for something I did not do. I did not kill Daniel Seifert and also I did not have anything to do with it.'

He was right. He did get life. It was 33 years to the day since Daniel Seifert had been killed. His son Joseph was in the courtroom. It was his turn to laugh.

The Chicago Outfit

Unlike the 'Five Families' who compete for turf in New York, the Chicago Outfit runs all organized crime in the city. But like all Italian-American crime families it is still answerable to the Commission.

Also known as the Chicago Crime Syndicate, the Outfit started in 1919 when a Black Hand gang under 'Sunny Jim' Cosmano tried to shake down a chain of brothels run by 'Big Jim' Colosimo. At this, Colosimo called for back-up from his wife's cousin Johnny Torrio, a saloon and brothel keeper in New York. Within a month, 18 of Cosmano's gang had been gunned down. Cosmano himself was wounded by a shotgun blast and fled the city.

Torrio had brought with him a New Yorker of Neapolitan descent named Al Capone. With Prohibition now in force, Torrio wanted to go into bootlegging. Colosimo was against it, so he too was gunned down.

The largely Irish North Side Gang were Torrio's rivals in the bootlegging business. Their attempt on Torrio's life left him badly wounded and he returned to Italy, leaving Capone in charge.

Al Capone, the most famous mobster of all time

Capone expanded the Outfit, wiping out George 'Bugs' Moran, Earl 'Hymie' Weiss and all who opposed him. He also introduced the principle that, unlike the New York families, you did not have to be Italian to join.

When Capone went to jail for tax evasion in 1931, his underboss Frank Nitti took over. But he was only a frontman. Former Neapolitan Camorrista Paul 'the Waiter' Ricca was acknowledged as boss by the Commission and ran the Outfit for the next 40 years.

Together Nitti and Ricca moved in on Hollywood. The studios paid them off to avoid labour unrest. But in 1943 they were indicted. Nitti shot himself rather than go to prison. Ricca then became the official boss with his enforcer Tony 'Big Tuna' Accardo as underboss. Accardo was also dubbed 'Joe Batters' by Capone after he killed two men with a baseball bat while Capone looked on.

After three years in jail, Ricca took a back seat, leaving Accardo as acting boss. Meanwhile the Outfit took in new recruits including Fiore 'Fifi' Buccieri and Salvatore 'Sam' Giancana, who helped Frank Sinatra build his career. Giancana also gave his support to John F. Kennedy, who was elected as US president in 1960.

With the aid of union leader Jimmy Hoffa and old-time mobster Meyer Lansky, Accardo used the Teamsters' pension fund and the Outfit's casinos to launder money. Accardo was officially a *consigliere* until his death in 1992, but ran the Outfit using a series of front bosses, who included Giancana, Samuel 'Teets' Battaglia, Jackie 'the Lackey' Cerone, Joseph 'Joey Doves' Aiuppa, Joseph 'Joe Nagall' Ferriola and Sam 'Wings' Carlisi.

John 'No Nose' DiFronzo - aka 'Johnny Bananas' - took over in 1993, followed by Angelo J. 'the Hook' LaPietra, who got his soubriquet from his method of torturing his victims. He would hang them on a meat hook then burn them with a blowtorch. During that era Lombardo was either underboss, *consigliere*, or - some say - the real boss of the Chicago Outfit.

JOE BATTERS

Name: *Antonino Joseph 'Tony' Accardo*

Aka: *Big Tuna, Joe Batters*

Born: *28 April 1906, Chicago, USA*

Died: *22 May 1992, Barrington Hills, Illinois*

Gang affiliation: *the Chicago Outfit*

Charges: *Illegal gambling, carrying a concealed weapon, disorderly conduct, mail fraud*

Tony Accardo came to fame as Al 'Scarface' Capone's enforcer. Capone was impressed when he watched Accardo kill two would-be traitors with a baseball bat, saying: 'But this kid's a real Joe Batters.' However, Accardo was also respected for his intelligence. It was said that he had 'more brains before breakfast than Al Capone had all day'. In a criminal career that lasted over 70 years, he never did any time in jail.

Accardo's parents were from Sicily, emigrating to the United States the year before he was born. He grew up on Chicago's West Side. Dropping out of school at 14, he became a delivery boy for a florist, then a clerk in a grocery store. These were the only two legitimate jobs he had in his lifetime.

His first arrest – for a motor vehicle violation – came in 1922. The following year, he was fined $200 for disorderly conduct in a pool hall where gangsters hung out. Two more convictions for disorderly conduct brought him to the attention of Al Capone, then well on his way to becoming Chicago's crime czar.

Accardo joined the Circus Café Gang, whose members included 'Screwy' Claude Maddox, Anthony 'Tough Tony' Capezio and Vincenzo DeMora, aka 'Machine Gun' Jack McGurn. The gang became allied to Capone's Chicago Crime Syndicate.

After delivering moonshine from the home stills in Little Sicily to the speakeasies around Chicago, Accardo quickly graduated to pick-pocketing, mugging, auto theft, burglary, assault and armed robbery, and was arrested several times.

CAPONE'S HITMAN

DeMora graduated to Capone's inner circle as a hitman and when Capone sought to expand his crew he recommended Accardo, who quickly showed his usefulness by saving Capone's life. When an assassination attempt was made by the North Side Mob, Accardo pulled Capone down and shielded him with his body. As a result, he became his personal bodyguard.

In later years, Accardo boasted of participating in the St Valentine's Day Massacre, where seven members of Bugs Moran's North Side Gang were wiped out. Although he was never officially tied to the murders, he was seen in the lobby of the Lexington Hotel on Michigan Avenue – Capone's headquarters – with a machine gun. Accardo was arrested soon afterwards, but no one was ever charged. He certainly carried out other hits for Capone.

When two of the other gunmen, Giovanni Scalise and Alberto Anselmi, tried to take over, Capone invited them to a formal dinner with other gangsters. After the speeches, Accardo beat them to death with a baseball bat. This was the occasion on which he earned his soubriquet.

PLAYING THE SLOTS

When Capone went to jail for income-tax evasion in 1931, Accardo was given his own gang that helped run gambling in Chicago and Florida. He quickly rose to number seven in the Chicago Crime Commission's 'public enemy' list.

Paul 'the Waiter' Ricca took over the Chicago Outfit in 1943, naming his friend Tony Accardo as his underboss. Together they ran the mob until Ricca's death in 1972, expanding their operations to Texas, Arizona, Nevada, Colorado and California, as well as Florida, Cuba and the Bahamas. They also pulled out of areas such as labour racketeering, which were attracting too much attention from the authorities. Instead the Outfit moved into slot machines, which appeared in petrol stations, restaurants and bars in the area controlled by the Outfit, as well as in the casinos in Las Vegas.

SINATRA'S CONTRIBUTION

In 1946, Accardo headed the Outfit's delegation to the meeting of the Commission called by Meyer Lansky in Havana. They took over the top four floors of the Hotel Nacional. Lucky Luciano was there. Delegates paid tribute with envelopes stuffed with cash, totalling $200,000, which Luciano said he would invest in the Nacional's casino. Frank Sinatra flew in to Cuba with Accardo, it is said, carrying a suitcase containing a million dollars for Luciano.

In 1957, Accardo was at the historic Mafia summit at Apalachin, upstate New York, to divide up the operations of Albert Anastasia following his assassination. It was held on the country estate of Joseph 'Joe the Barber' Barbara. However, the police noticed a large number of expensive cars with out-of-state license plates turning up and so they staged a raid. Accardo and Sam Giancana fled through the woods. Giancana later complained that he tore up a $1,200 suit on some barbed wire and ruined a new pair of shoes.

For some time in the late 1950s and early 1960s, Giancana handled the day-to-day running of the Outfit. He had begun his career in the mob as Accardo's driver and they had been arrested together for questioning in a kidnapping case. But his connection with John F. Kennedy gave him too high a profile to be boss, so Ricca and Accardo stepped in and deposed him.

KEEPING HIS HAND IN

Even while Giancana was in charge, Accardo still kept his hand in as an enforcer. He was thought to have been

> ## *A cattle prod was applied to his genitals and his body was punctured with ice-picks*

responsible for the killing of William 'Action' Jackson, a juice man or debt collector for the mob, who had possibly become an FBI informant. Jackson was stripped naked and beaten with a baseball bat and then he was hung by his rectum from a meat hook. His knees were broken, a cattle prod was applied to his genitals and his body was punctured with ice-picks. Then he was left for three days before he died.

When Ricca died, Accardo brought in his buddy Joe Aiuppa, who had been boss of the rackets in Cicero. Meanwhile Accardo began to spend more

time with his wife Clarice, a Polish-American former chorus girl, in their 22-room mansion – which boasted two bowling alleys, an indoor swimming pool, a pipe organ, a tub carved from a single piece of Mexican onyx and gold-plated bathroom fittings said to be worth half-a-million dollars.

CHAMPAGNE LIFESTYLE

The Internal Revenue Service investigated Accardo and in 1960 he was convicted of tax evasion, specifically for deducting $3,994 as operating expenses for his sports car, a red Mercedes-Benz 300SL. Accardo claimed to have used the car in the course of his employment as a salesman for a Chicago beer company. The jury found this hard to believe and convicted him. He was fined $15,000, and sentenced to six years in prison. The conviction was overturned on appeal.

Accardo did little to hide his personal wealth. He

Singer and actor Frank Sinatra (second from left) with Carlo Gambino (second from right) at a gathering in September 1976.

Tony Accardo's daughter, Linda, at her wedding to Michael Palermo in 1961: the wedding was such a lavish affair that one investigator later wrote if you were an Outfit guy and didn't get an invitation, you had a problem.

had lavish parties at his palatial home, with fountains gushing champagne and violinists mingling with the guests. He also enjoyed country sports. A phalanx of Cadillacs would take Accardo and his cronies out to South Dakota, where they would shoot pheasants with machine guns. And he got his nickname 'Big Tuna' for a 400-pound fish he caught.

Accardo also liked indoor sports. Once he was taken for $1,000 by a pool hustler who wedged the table and tweaked his game accordingly. When the trick was spotted, Accardo blamed himself for being such an easy dupe.

'Let the bum go,' he ordered. 'He cheated me fair and square.'

Accardo appeared before US Senate committees three times, carrying a cane with a tuna-fish handle. During his testimony, he invoked the Fifth Amendment, which protected citizens against self-incrimination, 172 times – including in answer to the question: 'Have you any scruples against killing?' He continued to deny any involvement in organized crime, while admitting that he knew leading figures in the Mafia. The only time he admitted breaking the law was years before when he had gambled.

Under investigation for labour racketeering, Accardo takes the oath before the Senate Government Affairs Committee.

WRONG HOUSE BURGLED

In January 1977, while Accardo was away, his home was broken into by some foolhardy burglars. When Accardo was told, he ordered Tony Spilotro, Aiuppa's most savage enforcer, to handle the case. The word got out and thieves and cat burglars fled the city, fearing they may be mistaken for the culprits. It took some time for Spilotro's men to crack the case, but this only made things worse because Accardo's temper continued to escalate.

Then a year after the break-in, Cook County began to reverberate with what they called 'trunk music'. The first burglar was found shot dead, another had been castrated and a third had had his face burned off with an acetylene torch. In each case, the coup de grace had been delivered with a bullet to the head or a slashed throat. For good measure, two of the executioners had also been killed. There were no further break-ins at Accardo's property.

Accardo died at the age of 86 of natural causes, a rare thing for a crime boss. He now lies in a mausoleum at the Queen of Heaven Cemetery in the Chicago suburb of Hillside, Illinois.

The St Valentine's Day Massacre

In 1929, Al Capone's only rival in Chicago was the Irish-American North Side Gang under Bugs Moran. Capone was determined to take over its rackets, so he cooked up a plan. He got a Detroit gangster to offer Moran a consignment of hijacked alcohol. The whiskey was to be delivered to the gang's headquarters, the garage of the SMC Cartage Company on 2122 North Clark Street, on 14 February.

Six of Moran's top men were waiting at the garage when Capone's men arrived, some disguised as policemen. Inside, the gunmen put Moran's men up against the wall and machine-gunned them. The men in uniform then escorted the other gunmen out of the garage as if they were being arrested.

When the police arrived, top Moran gunman Frank Gusenberg, who had tried to assassinate Capone three years earlier, was still alive. Although he knew he was going to die, he refused to talk. But there was little doubt about who was responsible. Moran said: 'Only Capone kills like that.'

As uniformed men had been seen at the garage, the police feared they might be implicated, so they turned their maximum efforts towards solving the crime. They quickly found what remained of the Cadillac the gunmen had used. It was in a burnt-out garage belonging to friends of Capone. 'Machine Gun' Jack McGurn was arrested. McGurn claimed to have been with his girlfriend at the time, but the prosecutor did not believe him and he was charged with perjury. Undaunted, he married his girlfriend so she could not be forced to testify against him.

Giovanni Scalise and Tony Accardo were also picked up, but there was no evidence against them. No one was ever charged with the St Valentine's Day Massacre and the case remains officially unsolved.

When asked who he thought was responsible, Capone suggested Bugs Moran. Afterwards he held a party so the celebrities there could watch the world title fight. Moran was now a spent force and Capone took over his operation. While before the massacre Capone had been regarded as a bootlegger, he was now seen as a cold-blooded killer.

The aftermath of the St Valentine's Day Massacre of 14 February 1929

THE PIG

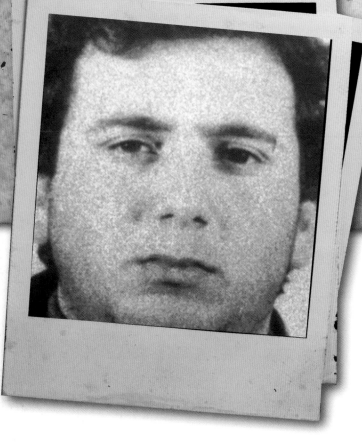

Name: *Giovanni Brusca*

Aka: *the Pig, the Butcher, the People-Slayer*

Born: *20 February 1957, San Giuseppe Jato, Sicily*

Clan affiliation: *Corleone*

Convictions: *Murder*

Giovanni Brusca is known quite simply as 'the Pig' for his unkempt appearance and unbridled appetites, which include a thirst for blood. He once admitted killing at least a hundred people, but couldn't remember the precise body count; he tortured and murdered the 11-year-old son of a fellow Mafioso who had turned state's evidence; and he also detonated the bomb that killed crusading prosecutor Giovanni Falcone, resulting in a huge anti-Mafia backlash. Then Brusca turned state's evidence himself.

There was never any doubt that Brusca would become a Mafioso. In the 1940s, his grandfather had given refuge to Salvatore Giuliano, the bandit and fugitive leader of the Movement for the Independence of Sicily. His father, Bernardo Brusca, had risen through the ranks to become a local boss. The young Giovanni Brusca first set foot in a prison at the age of five when his father was in jail. Bernardo would eventually serve several life sentences for his numerous killings and died in prison in the year 2000.

At the age of 12, on the instructions of his father, Brusca was delivering food and clothing to fugitives, including Bernardo Provenzano and Leoluca Bagarella, who were hiding out near his home in San Giuseppe Jato, a town halfway between Palermo and Corleone.

COLD BEFORE A MURDER

A local woman who had known Brusca as a youth said: 'He was a very normal teenager. He went out for pizza and to discotheques like everybody else.'

However, his free time was usually spent cleaning his father's weapons which were kept buried in the fields.

At 18 he was already overweight and had sloping shoulders. It was then that he committed his first murder. He was not told why the person had to die, but he and two others loosed a hail of bullets as the mark drove by. The victim was fatally wounded and died later in hospital.

The following year, Brusca ambushed a thief who had challenged the Mafia's authority. When the miscreant came out of the cinema, Brusca carefully fired into the crowd with a double-barrelled shotgun, hitting only his target. Rushing home, he hid the gun, changed his clothes, and raced back to relish the mayhem he had caused.

'I've always been very cold before, during and after the crime,' he confided in his memoirs. 'I might sometimes be reluctant to become "operative". But once I'd decided, all the worries, the fears and the doubts disappeared.'

At 19, he was fast-tracked into the organization and initiated by Totò Riina himself, whom Brusca already called *padrino* or 'godfather'. He then went to work as a driver for Bernardo Provenzano.

Mafia turncoat Tommaso Buscetta remembered the young Brusca as 'a wild stallion but a great leader'. Another informant, Salvatore Barbagallo, said: 'Giovanni was an excellent soldier, but he doesn't know how to think politically.' But mostly he was remembered as a ruthless butcher with little charisma.

NEVER UPSET BY TORTURE

In his memoirs, Brusca himself admitted: 'I've tortured people to make them talk; I've strangled both those who confessed and those who remained silent; I've dissolved bodies in acid; I've roasted corpses on big grills; I've buried the remains after digging graves with an earthmover. Some *pentiti* say today they feel disgust for what they did. I can speak for myself: I've never been upset by these things.'

Brusca's torture sessions would usually last for only half an hour. He would break the victim's legs with a

The aftermath of the Falcone bombing, 24 May 1992

hammer and pull his ears with pliers – 'but only enough to hurt him and make him understand that we were serious'. This was rarely effective, because the victims knew that they were going to be killed anyway.

'The condemned showed superhuman strength,' he said. 'We realized that and we'd say the fateful word: "*Niscemuninne*" ("Let's get out of here"). The torturers would then strangle the victim.'

Brusca did not even have to know his victims. Once a boss from the neighbourhood of Agrigento asked him for a favour – to kill anyone on a certain type of tractor, in a certain place, at a certain time. Three tractors drove by and he killed all three drivers. On another occasion, he rushed a job because the victim was about to get married and he did not want to leave the would-be wife a widow.

THE MURDER OF FALCONE

During the Second Mafia War in the early 1980s, Brusca became a member of Riina's death squad, which introduced terrorist tactics. He would travel escorted by a truck containing men carrying AK-47s. If they were stopped by the police and the back doors were opened for a routine check, they were told to open fire immediately.

In July 1983, the death squad blew up Palermo chief prosecutor Rocco Chinnici outside his home. The car bomb they used also killed Chinnici's two bodyguards and the porter of the apartment block and injured another 20 people. The car itself was blown three stories high, before crashing back to earth.

Two weeks after the murder of Chinnici, Riina ordered Brusca to prepare another car bomb. This time the target was to be Giovanni Falcone, who was working on indictments for what would become the Maxi Trial, where Riina would be sentenced, *in absentia,* to life.

Brusca tried to keep watch on Falcone's home but, following Chinnici's assassination, the police were stopping anyone parking outside the homes of prosecutors or other prominent officials. Instead Brusca stationed himself outside the law courts, where he noticed a truck that brought coffee and pastries to the prosecutors each morning. He planned to pack an identical truck with explosives, but could not work out how to make his getaway without being caught in the blast, so Riina told him to leave it for another time.

His next target was Salvatore Lima, a former mayor of Palermo who had become a member of the Italian chamber of deputies. He was in the firing line for having failed to protect Mafiosi from the Maxi Trial or use his influence to get their convictions overturned on appeal. Lima was on his way to make arrangements for a dinner in honour of former Italian prime minister Giulio Andreotti, who was visiting Palermo, when gunmen on motorcycles blew the tyres out on his car. Lima tried to escape on foot but was shot through the head.

Brusca was then contracted to kill Falcone. The judge had made the mistake of falling into a routine. Every Saturday he would fly in from Rome with his wife, then drive down the autostrada to their home near Palermo. The original plan was to blow up a bridge on the freeway, but Brusca thought that it would not work. He also vetoed a plan to blow up a pedestrian underpass, because the main force of the blast would come out of the exits. Instead he chose to pack the explosives into a narrow metal drainpipe that ran under the road near the exit to Capaci. The bomb would be detonated by a remote control device normally used in conjunction with model aircraft. Brusca tested it by setting off old-fashioned flash bulbs, working out precisely when he had to flick the switch to blow up a speeding car.

Simulations were performed on a quiet country road outside Corleone. Metal tubes were buried and concreted over to see just how effective the explosives were going to be. After successful tests, Brusca reported back to Riina that he was 'operational'.

Twelve drums containing 770 pounds of explosive in all were placed under the freeway, transported beneath the road on a skateboard. Then for weeks Brusca and his men kept watch, looking out for Falcone. Twice they

There was a huge explosion that registered on the earthquake monitor on the other side of the island

missed him. Once he was with his friend and fellow prosecutor Paolo Borsellino.

'If we'd known, we'd have killed two birds with one stone,' said Brusca.

But on the afternoon of 23 May 1992, Falcone and his wife Francesca were spotted by Mafia lookouts while driving down the autostrada that runs along the coast, after leaving Punta Raisi airport. Their armour-plated car was one of a convoy of three. Brusca flicked the switch to the remote control. There was a huge explosion that registered on the earthquake monitor on the other side of the island. The first car was blasted into an olive grove 60 yards away, killing the three bodyguards inside. Falcone's car teetered on the edge of a huge crater in the road. The judge, his wife and their driver were badly injured.

Falcone was heard to say: 'If I survive, this time I'll make them pay . . . '

He and his wife died shortly after they arrived in hospital. Only the driver survived.

When Brusca arrived back in Palermo, the television news channels were still reporting that Falcone was fighting for his life.

'That cuckold, if he doesn't die he will make life hell for us,' said Brusca.

Then came the news flash: 'Falcone is dead.'

Brusca was paid handsomely and celebrated with champagne.

Mafia boss Salvatore Riina following his arrest in Palermo, 15 January 1993

Burned-out cars litter the street following the bomb attack that killed Paolo Borsellino as he pulled up outside his mother's house in Palermo on 19 July 1992.

CRACKDOWN

The murder of Falcone and, soon after, Borsellino provoked an unprecedented crackdown on the Mafia. In January 1993, Riina was arrested after 23 years as a

> **Brusca strangled the boy with his bare hands and threw his body into a vat of acid**

fugitive. Brusca, Bagarella and Provenzano decided to continue the war against the state that Riina had begun. They discussed poisoning children's snacks, planting HIV-infected syringes on the beaches of Rimini and toppling the Leaning Tower of Pisa. Instead they opted for a series of bomb attacks.

First a bomb went off in Rome which aimed to kill TV host Maurizio Costanzo, who had rejoiced at the arrest of Riina. Costanzo was unhurt, but 23 bystanders were injured. Two weeks later a bomb exploded outside the Uffizi Gallery in Florence, killing five, wounding 40 and damaging dozens of priceless works of art. The following month, there was an attack on the Gallery of Modern Art in Milan, followed by another on Rome's Basilica of St John Lateran, killing another five people. Then a bomb was planted in the Olympic Stadium in Rome. It was timed to go off during a soccer match, but it failed to detonate.

Mario Santo Di Matteo, one of Brusca's accomplices in the Falcone bombing, was arrested and became a *pentito*. Brusca sent six of his soldiers to kidnap Di Matteo's 11-year-old son Giuseppe. They were dressed as policemen and told the boy they were taking

him to see his father. Giuseppe, whom Brusca knew personally, was held for 18 months and tortured. Grisly photographs were sent to his father in an attempt to make him recant. In the end, Brusca strangled the boy with his bare hands and threw his body into a vat of acid.

Following the murder of more relatives of Mafia informants – and direct attacks on the Church and Italy's vaunted artistic heritage – the race to capture Brusca was on. He began disguising himself, either sporting a beard or moustache or shaving his head. With his girlfriend Rosaria and their five-year-old son, Brusca frequently moved hideouts and sent coded messages, to avoid using the phone. In January 1996, police swooped on a villa near Palermo to find Brusca gone, but his dinner still warm on the table.

INTERRUPTED TV DINNER

Then Brusca grew careless. Having moved to Agrigento on the southern coast of Sicily, he was using a mobile phone to conclude a million-dollar drugs shipment when a plainclothes policeman rode through the neighbourhood on a scooter without a silencer. This enabled police phone tappers to pinpoint his hideout.

Two hundred black-hooded men from the anti-Mafia squad surrounded the house. They burst in to find Brusca eating a steak and, ironically, watching a TV movie about the Falcone killing. He also had a copy of Falcone's book on the Cosa Nostra.

Brusca quickly turned state's evidence. The prosecutor supplied him with a list of unsolved murders and Brusca went through it, ticking those he was responsible for. He was sentenced to life imprisonment, which was then reduced to 26 years as a reward for this collaboration. Then, in 2004, a court ruled that he should be let out for a week every 45 days to visit his wife and son.

Giovanni Falcone and Paolo Borsellino

Investigating magistrates Giovanni Falcone and Paolo Borsellino were both born in Palermo and joined the Antimafia Pool created there in the early 1980s by Judge Rocco Chinnici. Falcone worked in the bankruptcy section and became an expert in forensic accounting. His cases depended on financial records, so there were no witnesses who could be intimidated. He only prosecuted cases which could be heard before a tribunal of three judges, so there were no jurors who could be bought. Combing though five years of bank records, he managed to prove that the Spatola Construction Company was a front for drug smuggling, and obtained 74 convictions in all.

Falcone (left) and Borsellino, who said: 'Giovanni is my shield against the Cosa Nostra. They'll kill him, then they'll kill me.'

Borsellino concentrated on prosecuting the killers of Captain Emanuele Basile, an officer in the *carabinieri* who had issued 55 warrants on drug charges to members of the Bontade and Inzerillo families. But the judge declared a mistrial, allowing the suspects back on to the street. Fearing for his safety, Chinnici removed Borsellino from Mafia investigations. But when Chinnici was murdered, his successor Antonino Caponetto let Falcone and Borsellino work together and share information with other investigating magistrates. Then, in 1983, a new minister of justice in Rome provided them with computers to deal with the huge amounts of financial data they had to handle.

Together with information supplied by *pentiti*, evidence unearthed by Falcone and Borsellino was used in the Maxi Trial, where 475 defendants faced trial in a specially built courtroom bunker near Ucciardone prison in Palermo. It ran from February 1986 to December 1987 and over a thousand witnesses were called. In all, 344 of the defendants were found guilty and sentenced to a total of 2,665 years in jail, not counting the 19 life sentences that had been handed down to the most important bosses in Sicily, including – *in absentia* – Totò Riina and Bernardo Provenzano.

Riina ordered Brusca to kill Falcone. After a bomb was found in Falcone's beach house, he was transferred to Rome where he continued to fight organized crime. However, his weekly commute from Sicily to Rome took him along the coastal freeway, where his car was blown up on 23 May 1992.

Borsellino was at Falcone's bedside when he died. Afterwards he went to inspect the site of the explosion; he knew he was next. For Borsellino, investigating the Mafia was now a race against time. A *pentito* named Vincenzo Calcara told him: 'We were to shoot you with a rifle equipped with a telescopic sight – a real professional job. They had chosen me as the killer. They even gave me the weapon.'

On the afternoon of 19 July 1992, Borsellino called his mother to tell her that he was coming to visit her. When he reached her house, a car bomb exploded outside, killing him and his five bodyguards and wounding 18 people. There was damage to the apartment block as high as the 11th floor and it took the police a week to remove human remains from the street.

There is a memorial to the two judges at Palermo International airport, which was renamed Falcone-Borsellino airport in their honour.

A memorial to Borsellino, Falcone and his wife, Francesca Morvillo, in Palermo

THE SIXTH FAMILY

Name: *Vincenzo Cotroni*

Aka: *Vincent Cotroni, Vic Catrone, Vic Vincent, the Egg*

Born: *10 October 1911, Mammola, Calabria, Italy*

Died: *19 September 1984, Montreal, Canada*

Gang affiliation: *Bonanno*

Charges: *rape, theft, possessing counterfeit money, receiving stolen goods, felonious assault, conspiracy, trafficking narcotics*

Vincenzo 'the Egg' Cotroni was 14 years old when his family emigrated from Calabria to Montreal. They lived in a shabby apartment at Saint-Timothée in Ontario. Cotroni did not attend school in Canada. Instead, he worked as an assistant to his father, a carpenter, then became a professional wrestler under the name Vic Vincent.

With his brothers Francesco – 'Frank' – and Giuseppe – 'Peppe' or 'Pep' – he became a petty criminal. By the time he was 20 he had built up a long rap sheet that included minor crimes such as theft, possessing counterfeit money, the illegal sale of alcohol, and assault and battery. He was also charged with the rape of Maria Bresciano, but she dropped the charge and became his wife. They had a daughter and stayed together until Maria's death, though Cotroni also had a son with his French-Canadian mistress, a teacher.

DRUGS ON THE MARKET

The three brothers moved into bootlegging, prostitution, gambling and drugs. By 1945, they had become powerful enough to use extortion to buy votes and intimidate officials at polling stations during elections. This brought them to the attention of Joseph 'Joe Bananas' Bonanno, who had taken over the Maranzano family in 1931 and made it the Bonanno family. He sent his underboss Carmine Galante to

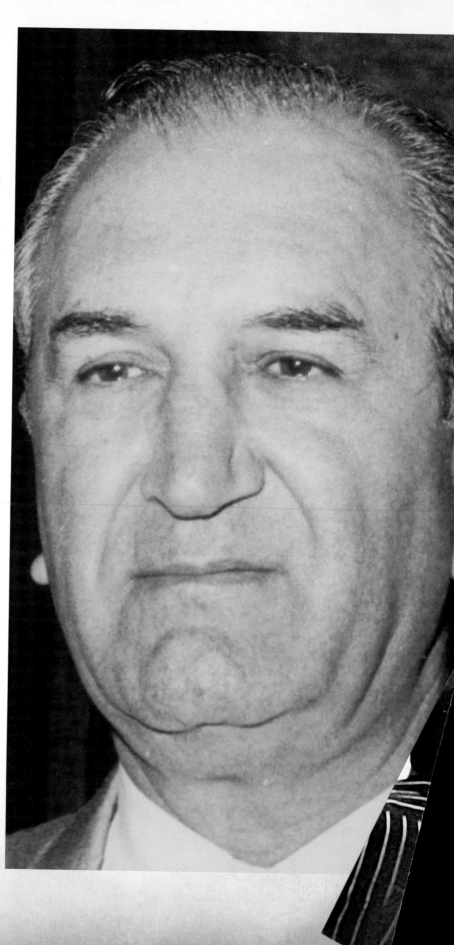

'Joe Bananas' Bonanno at a federal court hearing in June 1966, two years after his disappearance in 1964. FBI recordings captured angry Bonanno soldiers saying, 'That son-of-a-bitch took off and left us here alone.'

Montreal, which was to become the hub of the Bonanno family's narcotics importing business.

Galante soon found there were restaurants and nightclubs that had not been shaken down thoroughly enough and pimps, prostitutes, madams, back-alley abortionists, illegal gambling houses and after-hours lounges who were paying a mere pittance. So he imposed a 'street tax' on them. Cotroni and Galante grew close and Vic became godfather to one of Galante's children.

The drugs operation ran smoothly. Later a government witness, a little-known criminal named Edward Smith, described meetings with Galante and Vic, Pep and Frank Cotroni. In a Montreal apartment, Galante would open a suitcase on the coffee table. Smith's partner would count the bags of white powder inside and Smith would take the suitcase to Frank's Bar & Grill in Brooklyn, where the contents would be cut and distributed.

In 1956, the Canadian authorities began to crack down on American gangsters in their midst and Galante became a target because of his strong-arm tactics. Notorious for his cruelty, Galante would smash beer glasses on the floor in a restaurant he owned and make a busboy dance barefoot on the shards. Galante was deported to the United States. His associate Salvatore 'Little Sal' Giglio, who set up the drugs pipeline between

Marseilles and Montreal, was caught with 240 Cuban cigars and 800 American cigarettes he had failed to declare and similarly ousted.

THE GOOD LIFE

The Bonannos' Montreal interests were left in the hands of Vic Cotroni and the Sicilian Luigi 'Louie' Greco. According to Joe's son, Salvatore 'Bill' Bonanno: 'Cotroni was the head honcho. He was captain of the crew. Louie was his right-hand man. We had to have a couple of sit-downs to straighten that out, but we got it down. They trusted and listened to my dad . . . Louie was big enough to respect that. Louie knew it was best for everyone . . . If any of Louie's guys made trouble, Louie knew he had New York to answer to.'

In 1959, Pep Cotroni pleaded guilty to drug trafficking and was jailed for ten years. Galante was also arrested. The trial was repeatedly delayed; one postponement occurred when one of the defendants absconded the day before the trial was scheduled.

In this FBI surveillance photo taken in September 1977, Bonanno soldier Anthony Mirra speaks to another family member.

Cotroni could neither read nor write, but in the 1960s he owned a limousine, along with a duplex in Rosemont and a house outside the city in Lavaltrie. This had marble floors, six bathrooms, a huge conference room, a walk-in refrigerator, crystal chandeliers and a cinema. He was also a pillar of the community, making large donations to Montreal churches and various charities.

INFLUENCING THE JURY

After six months of what an appeal court judge would later call 'every conceivable type of obstruction and interruption', Galante's trial was halted on the eve of the summations to the jury. The foreman of the jury had broken his back. He seemed to have fallen down the stairs of an abandoned building in the middle of the night.

A retrial in 1962 began with one of the defendants, Salvatore Panico, shouting abuse before the jury had even been selected. Panico would later clamber into the jury area to rough up the front row while screaming abuse at them and the judge. Then Anthony Mirra, another Bonanno soldier – who was later whacked for introducing 'Donnie Brasco' Pistone to the family – picked up the witness chair and flung it at the prosecutor. This did not help their case and Galante was sentenced to 20 years.

KEEPING A LOW PROFILE

By now Cotroni had learned to keep a low profile and when *Maclean's* magazine referred to him as the godfather of Montreal, he sued for $1.25 million. However, the judge ruled that Cotroni's name was 'tainted' and awarded him $2 for the English-language edition of *Maclean's* and $1 for the French-language edition.

In the 1970s, Cotroni turned over the day-to-day running of the family to the hot-headed Paolo Violi, another immigrant from Calabria. In 1955 Violi had pumped four bullets into fellow immigrant Natale Brigante in a car-park row about a woman in their home country. Brigante died, but not before he had stabbed Violi under the heart. Violi showed the stab wound in court, claiming he had acted in self-defence. The manslaughter charge against him was then dropped.

In the early 1960s, Violi hooked up with Vic's younger brother, Frank 'Le Gros' Cotroni. He ran an extortion racket in the Italian community of St Leonard and then went into counterfeiting and bootlegging. In 1965, he married the daughter of Giacomo Luppino, a member of the 'Ndrangheta from Calabria who had become boss of Hamilton, Ontario. Vic Cotroni and Ontario mobsters Paul Volpe and Johnny 'Pops' Papalia were godfathers to their children. When an underworld figure was forced to give testimony before a government commission about Violi's standing, he said: 'My Lord, his name, it's like a god . . . everyone is afraid of him. Violi, he's not one man – he's a thousand men.'

SHARED TELEPHONE LINE

In 1973, war erupted between the Cotronis and the French-Canadian Dubois gang. On a wiretap, Violi was heard saying they should go into the Dubois' club, 'clients or no clients, line everybody up against the wall and rat-a-tat-tat'. Cotroni had a cooler head and persuaded him to make peace.

The following year, Cotroni was called before the Quebec Police Commission's inquiry into organized crime and was sentenced to a year in prison for giving testimony that was 'deliberately incomprehensible, rambling, vague, and nebulous'. His lawyers won a reversal, but not before he had spent several months in jail.

Cotroni and Violi were then caught on a further wiretap. They were threatening Papalia, who had used their names in a $300,000 extortion plot without notifying them or cutting them in. They demanded $150,000, but Papalia insisted that he had only netted $40,000. Cotroni was then heard to say: 'Let's hope so because, eh, we'll

Vic Cotroni (centre, white shirt) with his brother Frank (on the right) and Paolo Violi (left) in an Acapulco nightclub in 1970.

kill you.' The three men were sentenced to six years, but Cotroni and Violi had their convictions quashed on appeal.

After Luigi Greco was burnt to death in an accidental fire at his pizzeria, the Sicilian faction of the family under

> *Everyone is afraid of Violi . . . he's not one man – he's a thousand men*

Nicolo Rizzuto made a bid for power. On 14 February 1976, Violi's *consigliere* Pietro Sciara was gunned down leaving a cinema with his wife. They had just seen *The Godfather*.

The following year, Violi's brother Francesco was on the telephone when he received a shotgun blast to the face. Then he was finished off with a couple of bullets from a handgun.

LAST CADILLAC RIDE

Violi was in jail for contempt of court at the time, for refusing to testify to the Police Commission. When he got out, Nick Rizzuto sought sanctuary in Venezuela. But on 22 January 1978, Violi was playing cards in a bar

The family of reputed Mafia member Joe Di Maulo release doves following his funeral in Montreal on 14 November 2012. Di Maulo was shot in his driveway. Once considered a trusted associate of the Rizzuto family, Di Maulo was also close to Frank Cotroni.

when two masked men walked in. One put a 12-bore shotgun to the back of his head and pulled the trigger.

At Violi's funeral, 31 black Cadillacs carried tributes from mobsters in North America and Italy. Three Sicilians were jailed for the slaying.

For weeks afterwards, Cotroni stayed inside his fortress in Lavaltrie while Rizzuto took over the family. It seems Cotroni had at least approved the hit on Violi.

Vincenzo Cotroni died of cancer in 1984. There were only 23 cars carrying floral tributes at his funeral. However, 17 brass bands turned out to mark the passing of Montreal's legendary 'man of respect'. By then, Galante was dead and the Bonanno family was in decline, their links with the Cotronis severed. The Montreal mob was gearing up to become North America's 'sixth family'.

Vito Rizzuto

The son of Nicolo Rizzuto, Vito was born in 1946 in the Sicilian province of Agrigento and migrated with his family to Canada in 1954.

At the age of 19, Rizzuto Jr. was fined $25 for disturbing the peace. Then in 1972 he was sent to prison for two years for conspiracy to commit arson with his brother-in-law, Paolo Renda. When war broke out between the Calabrian and Sicilian factions of the Montreal mob and his father fled to Venezuela, Vito stayed behind. The war was finally over in 1981, with more than 20 casualties in Canada and Italy, and Nick and Vito Rizzuto emerged as leaders of the Montreal Mafia. Vito became his father's enforcer.

Michel Pozza, a financial adviser who had worked exclusively for Cotroni before the split, now saw the Sicilians as his best bet. But it was a bad move. A few days after he was seen talking to Rizzuto, Pozza was gunned down outside his Laurentian home.

In 1987, the Royal Canadian Mounted Police seized 16 tons of hashish with an estimated street value of $350 million on an island off the coast of Newfoundland. Rizzuto was arrested and charged with trafficking, but the charges were dropped when a Supreme Court judge ruled that the evidence had been obtained unlawfully. However, four other men went to jail.

While out on bail, Rizzuto was charged with smuggling 32 tons of Lebanese hashish into the country. He was acquitted when a witness named Normand Dupuis refused to testify. Dupuis later claimed that he had been offered $1 million not to take the stand, but had only made his decision after his family received death threats. Rizzuto walked free, while Dupuis was given 32 months for the obstruction of justice.

Vito Rizzuto took over the family in 1988 when his father went to jail in Venezuela for cocaine trafficking. Rizzuto Sr. was paroled in 1993 when Montreal mobster Domenic Tozzi delivered an $800,000 bribe to Venezuelan officials. Returning to Canada, he then became his son's business adviser.

In 2004, Vito Rizzuto was arrested again. After a 31-month battle he was extradited to the United States where he pleaded guilty to the 1981 killing of the rival Bonanno *capos*, alongside Big Joey Massino. This was part of a plea bargain and he was sentenced to just ten years.

He was released after only five years and deported back to Canada. By then his eldest son Nicolo had been gunned down; his father had been killed by a sniper who had shot him through his kitchen window; his brother-in-law and *consigliere* Paolo Renda had disappeared, believed dead; and his associate Agostino Cuntrera had been executed.

After Vito's release there have been 14 hits in Montreal, thought to have been in retaliation. Meanwhile Rizzuto lives in a well-guarded apartment in downtown Montreal and drives around in a $100,000 armoured car.

Montreal police walk past the house of Vito Rizzuto's father, crime boss Nicolo Rizzuto, Sr., who was shot dead by a sniper through his kitchen window in 2010 at the age of 86.

THE CHARNEL HOUSE

Name: *Roy Albert DeMeo*

Aka: *the Rooster*

Born: *7 September 1942, Bath Beach, Brooklyn*

Died: *10 January 1983, Brooklyn*

Gang affiliation: *Gambino*

Charges: *loan-sharking, auto theft, selling stolen cars, pandering, selling pornography, trafficking narcotics, tax evasion, murder*

A made man in the Gambino family, Roy DeMeo was one of the most feared hitmen in the mob. He killed over a hundred men and disposed of their bodies with assembly-line efficiency.

THE GEMINI METHOD

Victims would be lured to a charnel house called the Gemini Lounge in Brooklyn, where DeMeo and his gang of assassins hung out. Entering through a side door, they would be taken to an apartment at the back of the building. As soon as a victim walked in, he would be shot in the head using a gun with a silencer. A towel would quickly be wrapped around his head to catch the blood and someone would stab him in the heart to stop it pumping.

The body would then be dragged into the bathroom, put in the shower and drained of blood. Then the corpse would be laid out on a pool liner in the living room where DeMeo, who had been an apprentice butcher in his youth, had shown the crew how to take bodies apart bit by bit. The smaller the bits the better, because it hindered identification – the head would even be consigned to a rubbish compactor. The body parts would then be dumped at the huge Fountain Avenue landfill in Brooklyn, where it was unlikely that any trace of them would ever be discovered.

DeMeo enjoyed the business of dismembering his victims. Some, though, had to be left intact – as proof of death, for instance. All knew that an invitation to the Gemini Lounge was likely to be a death warrant.

ASSEMBLING THE TEAM

After dropping out of school at 17, DeMeo involved himself in legitimate businesses while making the bulk of his money from loan-sharking, which he had learned from the sons of local Mafia boss Joe Profaci. DeMeo had no qualms about using violence on those who did not pay up on time. Gambino associate Anthony 'Nino' Gaggi got to hear about him and invited him to his home. DeMeo knew of the Gambinos through family associations with the Lucchese and set his heart on becoming a member.

Under Gaggi, DeMeo set up his own crew with his cousin Joseph 'Dracula' Guglielmo, marijuana dealer Harvey 'Chris' Rosenberg, Anthony Senter, Freddy DiNome, 'Dirty' Henry Borelli and Joey and Patrick Testa. They loan-sharked, sold stolen cars and laundered drugs money through the Boro of Brooklyn Credit Union, after DeMeo had talked his way on to the board. Gaggi and DeMeo also muscled their way into the X-rated movie business.

BUTCHERED IN THE MEAT DEPARTMENT

When Andrei Katz, a body shop owner involved in a stolen car ring, testified to a grand jury, DeMeo decided that he had to go. The crew abducted him. Taking him to the meat department of a supermarket in Queens, they stabbed him in the heart, dismembered him, and dumped the remains beneath some rotting vegetables in a rubbish bin. But the body parts were discovered by a homeless man searching for food. Borelli and Joey Testa were arrested and tried, but acquitted. These were the early days, before the 'Gemini method' had been perfected. From then on, the crew decided to be more careful.

When their X-rated movie business was raided, Gaggi and DeMeo feared that one of their partners, Paul Rothenberg, might turn informer. DeMeo invited Rothenberg out to dinner and then shot him in the head in an alleyway.

When Carlo Gambino died and Paul Castellano took over, DeMeo expected promotion, particularly as Gaggi was close to Castellano. Gaggi put in a good word for DeMeo, but Castellano did not trust him and refused to make him a made man. However, when DeMeo arranged a lucrative alliance with the Westies, an Irish-American gang from Hell's Kitchen, Castellano finally gave in and gave DeMeo his 'button'.

DeMeo continued dealing in drugs, despite the Gambino family's rule against it, but by then he had become too useful as a hitman. He even used murder to discipline his own crew. Danny Grillo, a gambler who was heavily in debt to DeMeo, was disposed of in the Gemini Lounge.

STUDENT MAKES ERROR

Next to go was Chris Rosenberg, one of DeMeo's oldest associates. Introducing himself as Chris DeMeo, he had set up a cocaine deal in Florida. When a four-man team – including the girlfriend of the Cuban supplier known only as 'El Negro' – arrived in New York to deliver the drugs, Rosenberg had them shot and dismembered. But El Negro and his Cuban gang were well connected. They threatened a war with the Gambinos unless Rosenberg was very publicly killed.

DeMeo was reluctant to whack an old pal and procrastinated, but when the Cubans appeared in town he became paranoid. When an 18-year-old student named Dominick A. Ragucci, who was selling vacuum cleaners door-to-door to pay for his education, turned up outside his house, DeMeo took him for a Cuban hitman. He and Guglielmo came out wielding guns. Seeing them,

It's just like takin' apart a deer. It's only weird if you do it while the guy's still alive

Ragucci slammed his car into gear and sped away. The two gunmen jumped into DeMeo's Cadillac and chased after him, firing as they went.

At an intersection, Ragucci crashed into another car. Despite two flat tyres, Ragucci made it another 500 feet before his disabled vehicle shuddered to a halt. DeMeo then jumped from his Cadillac and emptied his pistol into the unfortunate teenager.

Gaggi then insisted that DeMeo kill Rosenberg before some other innocent civilian got hurt. So DeMeo shot Rosenberg in the head in the Gemini Lounge. But Rosenberg did not die immediately. As he rose to one knee, Sender finished him off with four more shots. To make sure the murder made the newspapers – so that El Negro would see it – the body was dumped in a car near the Gateway National Recreation Area and riddled with bullets, old style, with a Thompson sub-machine gun.

FAKE CHARITY AND THE FIRST LADY

But there was friction in the family, in the form of James Eppolito and his son James Eppolito Jr., two made men in the Gambino family. Eppolito Sr. told Paul Castellano that Gaggi and DeMeo were selling drugs. But Jimmy Jr. was out of favour with Castellano after he had appeared on *60 Minutes* with the First Lady, Rosalynn Carter, at a dinner for his crooked children's charity. If this was exposed, Castellano feared that President Jimmy Carter might react by sending a large contingent of FBI agents to New York to smash the Gambinos, so he gave Gaggi

and DeMeo permission to whack the Eppolitos. They were duly invited to the Gemini Lounge for a sit-down. Gaggi, DeMeo and Brooklyn wiseguy Peter 'Petey 17' Piacenti went to collect them. On the way, Jimmy Sr. wanted to stop so he could relieve himself. As he got out of the car on the service road of the Belt Parkway, Gaggi and DeMeo opened fire, killing both Eppolitos and putting a bullet through the windshield.

A witness alerted an off-duty police officer. As DeMeo made off, the officer approached Gaggi and Piacenti. Gaggi opened fire – and missed. The cop fired back, hitting Gaggi in the neck and Piacenti in the leg. They were arrested, but DeMeo had made his escape from the scene and was not implicated.

HITTING THE HIT MAN

Nevertheless, he was experiencing difficulties from another direction. He had expanded his auto-theft operation and was shipping stolen cars to Kuwait and Puerto Rico. However, his partner in the operation, Vito Arena, had been picked up and had agreed to turn state's evidence. This meant that DeMeo would have to appear before a grand jury. Castellano, who had never trusted DeMeo because of his thirst for murder, put out a hit on him. The problem was that DeMeo had such a fearsome reputation that even John Gotti turned down the contract.

Richard Kuklinski claims to have killed DeMeo. Other sources say that Gaggi put seven bullets in DeMeo's head in the Gemini Lounge. His body was dumped in the boot of his Cadillac and a chandelier he was taking to be repaired was placed on top of it. The car was then abandoned outside the Varnas Boat Club in Sheepshead Bay. A week later it was towed away by the police, who noticed dark stains on the seats. When they got it to the police garage they opened the boot and found the body.

Carlo Gambino's coffin is carried from Our Lady of Grace Roman Catholic church in Brooklyn on 18 October 1976. About 150 relatives and close friends, including top Mafia lieutenants, attended the funeral Mass for Gambino, 74, who died of a heart ailment at his home in Massapequa, New York.

Anthony Gaggi

Anthony 'Nino' Gaggi's father was a barber from Palermo. Nino was born in 1925 on the Lower East Side of Manhattan, where his mother was a seamstress in a sweatshop. As soon as he was able, Nino was put to work sweeping up and polishing shoes to make a little extra money during the Depression.

Joining a local street gang, he learned to fight alongside Rocky Graziano and Jake 'Raging Bull' LaMotta, both of whom went on to become world middleweight champions. Snatching fruit from barrows earned Gaggi a beating from the police which fuelled a festering contempt for the law that would last a lifetime.

Gaggi's mother had been a childhood friend of movie mobster George Raft, and Frank Scalise, a founder member of the Gambino family, was his father's cousin. As a child, Gaggi had a clear ambition. 'I only want two things when I grow up,' he said. 'I want to be just like Frank Scalise and, when I die, I want to die on the street with a gun in my hand.'

Loan-sharking operation

At 14, Gaggi quit school and went to work in his father's barber's shop. He also delivered flowers. With a little money in his pocket, he quickly learned that gambling was not for him - he could not stand to lose. Instead, he began loan-sharking.

Much to his dismay, his parents bought a farm in New Jersey and moved the family out there. At the age of 17, he tried to escape by enlisting in the army, but even though there was a war on, he was rejected because of his poor eyesight. Again this fuelled his resentment of authority.

His parents found that, as city people, they were not well suited to the farming life, so they moved back to Brooklyn, buying a house in the Italian area of Bath Beach. Gaggi got a job on a truck dock, quickly rising to become supervisor. He hated it but, thanks to Scalise, it became a ghost job. On paper he was an employee and had a legitimate income to show the Internal Revenue Service, but his real income came from loan-sharking.

Gaggi was unequivocal in his praise of his hero. 'Frank Scalise was the finest man I ever met,' he said. 'He was there with Luciano at the beginning of all this. Him and his brother Joe, they were two of the shooters on the St Valentine's hits in Chicago.'

In 1954 Gaggi was charged with running an auto-theft ring but when the case came to trial, witnesses mysteriously forgot what they had seen and he was acquitted.

Joins hit squad

With the murders of Scalise and Anastasia in 1957, Gaggi's associate Carlo Gambino took over the family. Then Gaggi joined the hit squad who killed Vincent Squillante, the man who was thought to have killed Frank Scalise and his brother Joe.

'We surprised him in the Bronx,' said Gaggi. 'We shot him in the head, then stuffed him in the trunk, drove to 10th Street, and threw him in a furnace.'

Having now killed, Gaggi became a made man. He then brought DeMeo and his crew into the family.

Although most of DeMeo's hits were for the family, Gaggi also pursued personal vendettas. Vincent Governara was one of a bunch of

Anthony Gaggi, who oversaw the Roy DeMeo crew of the Gambino family.

teenagers who had subjected Gaggi's sister-in-law to catcalls. When he waded into them with a hammer, Governara, a boxer, flattened him with a nose-breaking right hook. Afterwards, Governara sensibly moved away, but when he returned to Brooklyn 12 years later, Gaggi planted a concussion grenade in his car. Governara survived, but Gaggi and DeMeo then shot him down in the street in front of 20 bystanders.

On one occasion, Gaggi and his wife Rose were held at gunpoint while burglars ransacked their holiday home in Florida. Figuring that the thieves had been tipped off by electrical contractor George Byrum, who had done some work on the house, DeMeo lured Byrum to a hotel in Miami, shot him in the buttocks, then finished him off in front of Gaggi. They were cutting him up when they were interrupted by contractors fixing the hotel air-conditioning. The maid went into therapy after discovering the decapitated corpse.

After the Eppolito killings, Gaggi was shot in the neck by a police officer. As he collapsed, the gun flew from his hand. Despite being warned, Gaggi reached out for it anyway, but did not have the strength to lift it. The officer did not fire again, so Gaggi was denied his most cherished wish – to die in the street with a gun in his hand.

The officer who arrested him, and the witness who saw the killings, went into hiding and the jury was sequestered for the entire trial. However, one of the jurors was engaged to the son of one of Gaggi's loan-shark customers. Consequently, Gaggi was only found guilty of assault and sentenced to a term of 5–15 years. But the verdict was overturned after Gaggi told the juror under his control to make a false complaint of sexual misconduct about a court official. Just to make sure, DeMeo killed the witness, thereby preventing a retrial. While Gaggi was in jail, his nephew Dominick Montiglio became a drug addict and was arrested for loan-sharking. He then turned state's evidence. Vito Arena also testified against Gaggi. With DeMeo dead, the crew began to fall apart.

Gaggi stood trial for automobile theft and murder alongside Castellano and others. When Castellano was murdered, Gaggi was lead defendant. He was convicted of conspiracy to steal cars. While awaiting a second trial on racketeering and murder charges, he died of a heart attack, aged 52.

On 16 December 1985, police remove the blood-covered body of 'Big Paul' Castellano after he and his driver were gunned down outside Sparks Steak House by three men who fled on foot.

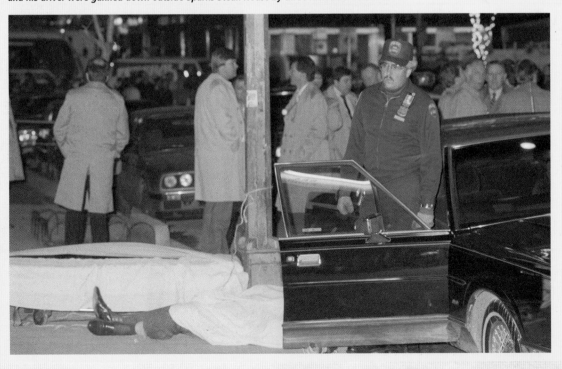

CASINO

Name: *Anthony Spilotro*

Aka: *Tony 'the Ant'*

Born: *19 May 1938, Chicago, Illinois*

Died: *14 June 1986, Enos, Indiana*

Gang affiliation: *Chicago Outfit*

Charges: *theft, murder, torture, illegal bookmaking, burglary*

After emigrating to Chicago from Puglia, Italy, in 1914, Anthony 'the Ant' Spilotro's parents ran Patsy's restaurant in Chicago, where such well known criminals as Frank Nitti, Paul 'the Waiter' Ricca and Sam Giancana regularly dined. Patsy's car park was often used for mob meetings.

Spilotro dropped out during his second year in high school and made money shoplifting and purse-snatching. Then he teamed up with childhood friend Frank Cullotta. They would rob Jewish kids and ride around together in stolen cars.

'Tony was the toughest kid I knew,' said Cullotta. 'He was so tough that his brother Victor used to offer guys $5 to see if they could beat him up. Usually, Victor got a taker and the guy would try to kick Tony's ass, but if it looked like Tony was gonna lose, we'd all jump on the kid and break his head.'

In a fight with some black boys, Spilotro pulled out a knife and stabbed one of them, but the victim did not press charges.

At the age of 17, Spilotro was fined $10 for stealing a shirt. He was arrested another 12 times for petty crimes before the age of 22.

When Cullotta and some other youths shot three men in a tavern, Spilotro helped them get rid of the guns. He then roped them into a scheme whereby they waited outside banks and robbed anyone carrying a large amount of cash.

By the age of 18, they were making $25,000 a month each. But when Cullotta bought a new Cadillac, Spilotro

*In Martin Scorsese's movie **Casino**, Joe Pesci (centre) plays Nicky Santoro,
a character based on Chicago mob enforcer Anthony Spilotro.*

told him to get rid of it. He had already made contact with the Chicago Outfit, who wanted them to continue driving around in inconspicuous Fords and Chevrolets.

ONE OF HIS EYES POPPED OUT

Spilotro hung out with Vinnie 'the Saint' Inserro, who introduced him to Jimmy 'the Turk' Torello, Charles 'Chuckie' Nicoletti, 'Milwaukee Phil' Alderisio, Joey 'the Clown' Lombardo and Joseph 'Joey Doves' Aiuppa, who would go on to become head of the Outfit – a job Spilotro had coveted from an early age.

On one occasion, two hold-up men named Bill McCarthy and Jimmy Miraglia had an argument with Philly and Ronnie Scalvo. The Scalvos were then found dead, along with a woman, but no one had given permission for the hit, so retribution was ordered.

Spilotro, Nicoletti and Alderisio abducted McCarthy. They took him to a workshop to torture him but he would not talk, even when they stabbed an ice-pick through his testicles. So Spilotro put McCarthy's head in a vice and tightened it until one of his eyes popped out. He then put lighter fuel on McCarthy's face and set fire to it. Unimpressed, Nicoletti ate pasta throughout.

Before he died, McCarthy gave up Miraglia's name. Eleven days later, the bodies of Miraglia and McCarthy were found in the boot of Miraglia's car.

Frank 'Lefty' Rosenthal adjusts his tie while refusing to answer questions before the Senate Rackets Subcommittee. Rosenthal was brought before the committee for bribery and match-fixing in 1961.

THE BOOKMAKING YEARS

After these murders, Spilotro hooked up with Outfit enforcer 'Mad' Sam DeStefano, collecting debts for him. As part of Milwaukee Phil's crew, he began shaking down bookies. Then he became a bail bondsman, bailing out soldiers for Lombardo, Alderisio and Torello.

By 1963, Spilotro was a made man in the Chicago Outfit, controlling the bookmaking in the northwest side of Chicago. He quickly attracted the attention of law enforcement officers and the media, who called him 'the Ant' because he was just 5 feet 2 inches tall.

The following year Spilotro was sent to Miami to work with childhood friend Frank 'Lefty' Rosenthal, a mob-backed bookmaker, handicapper and match-fixer.

In 1961, Rosenthal had appeared before the McClellan committee on Gambling and Organized Crime, where he took the Fifth Amendment 37 times – refusing even to say whether he was left-handed (the origin of his nickname).

JEWELLERY STORE HQ

In 1971, Spilotro was sent to run the Outfit's interests in Las Vegas. Again he worked with Rosenthal, who was in charge of the skim. His job was to siphon off as much cash as possible before it was recorded as revenue.

Working out of a jewellery store called The Gold Rush with his brother Michael, Spilotro imposed a street tax on all criminal activities, enforcing this with five murders where the victims were brutally tortured before they were killed. But even before Spilotro arrived in Las Vegas the FBI in Chicago had alerted the bureau there that he was on his way. He was only in town two weeks before they had a wiretap on him. The local police picked him up every three or four months 'on general principle'. It was a hassle, but Spilotro enjoyed the publicity.

REMOVING THE EVIDENCE

In September 1972, Spilotro had to go back to Chicago to face trial alongside 'Mad' Sam DeStefano and his brother, Mario, for the 1963 murder of real estate agent Leo Foreman. One of the killers, Charles 'Chuckie' Crimaldi, had turned state's evidence. Spilotro was also worried about fellow defendant Sam DeStefano who, it was said, had cancer and was afraid of dying in jail.

Spilotro and Mario DeStefano went to visit Sam on the pretext that they had discovered where Crimaldi was being held by the authorities. They told Sam they had bribed the guards to turn their backs while they whacked him. DeStefano was gloating about exacting his revenge on Crimaldi when his brother, Mario, stepped aside. Spilotro was standing behind him with a double-barrelled shotgun. One blast took off Mad Sam's arm. The

second hit him square in the chest, killing him instantly. Thanks to an alibi provided by his sister-in-law, Spilotro was acquitted in the Leo Foreman case and returned to Las Vegas.

Then Spilotro was indicted alongside Lombardo for defrauding the Teamsters' pension fund. This was solved by the murder of the only witness, 29-year-old Daniel Seifert. Both men were acquitted.

HOLE IN THE WALL GANG

Although Spilotro's job in Las Vegas was to keep an eye on Rosenthal and other Outfit interests, he began running a team of burglars known as the 'Hole in the Wall Gang', because they often gained entry by making a hole in a wall or roof.

Meanwhile, West Coast Mafia turncoat Aladena 'Jimmy the Weasel' Fratianno testified against him and

The victims were brutally tortured before they were killed

the Nevada Gaming Commission blacklisted Spilotro. He was barred from being physically present in any Nevada casino. As a result, he expanded the Hole in the Wall Gang's activities to encompass the entire tri-state area.

But the gang's burglar alarm specialist Sal Romano was picked up on another charge. He flipped, and the crew were arrested on their next outing. Hearing that there was a contract out on him, Cullotta also turned state's evidence, but his testimony was not enough to convict Spilotro on conspiracy charges.

FATAL AFFAIR

Nevertheless, the bosses of the Chicago Outfit were not pleased with Spilotro. As well as operating without their authority, he was gaining a dangerously high profile. Then came news that Spilotro was having an affair with Rosenthal's wife. Mafia bosses don't approve of such things. Rosenthal was then car-bombed. Although it was thought that Milwaukee boss Frank Balistrieri – aka the 'Mad Bomber' – was responsible, Spilotro was also a suspect. FBI wiretap evidence in which Spilotro mentioned Joseph 'Mr Clean' Ferriola, then running the Chicago Outfit, had also been heard in court.

Spilotro was about to face trial for skimming profits at the Stardust casino and violating the civil rights of a government witness he was thought to have murdered – not to mention a retrial of the Hole in the Wall case.

At the same time, Spilotro's brother, Michael, faced extortion charges in Chicago. On 14 June 1986, the two men were summoned to a meeting where they believed Michael was going to be a made man. Instead they were beaten with baseball bats and buried alive in a cornfield in Enos, Indiana, some 60 miles southeast of Chicago.

Their remains were accidentally unearthed by a farmer. The grave was just four miles from a hunting lodge owned by Mafia boss Joe Aiuppa, who was in prison at the time on charges of skimming profits from Las Vegas casinos.

Nicholas Pileggi's 1995 book, *Casino*, describes the Las Vegas careers of Spilotro and Rosenthal and was used as the basis for a movie of the same name directed by Martin Scorsese.

The first Mafia-financed casino of Las Vegas – the Flamingo – opened on 26 December 1946. By the 1950s, the mob's skim at the Stardust was $7 million a year. Mafia business continued to boom in Las Vegas until the 1980s.

Sam DeStefano

Born in southern Illinois, 'Mad' Sam DeStefano moved to Chicago as a teenager. At 18, he was convicted of rape. Convictions for extortion, bank robbery, assault with a deadly weapon and possessing counterfeit stamps soon followed.

In 1930, DeStefano joined Sam Giancana's West Side 42 gang of violent thugs and bootleggers. He rose to become a major drug trafficker and loan-shark – introducing the 'juice loan', where violence was used to force borrowers to repay.

While other 42 gang members rose to senior positions in the Chicago Outfit, DeStefano remained a debt collector and executioner. He kept his instruments of torture in the sound-proofed basement of his home, with his wife and three children living blissfully untroubled above.

Death by torture

When restaurant owner Artie Adler could not pay up, DeStefano took him to his basement and went to work on him with an ice-pick. During the torture Adler died of a heart attack. His body was dumped in a frozen sewer and caused a blockage during the spring thaw. This amused DeStefano no end.

Debt collector Peter Cappelletti tried to run off with $25,000. He was taken to Mario DeStefano's restaurant in Cicero, where he was stripped and handcuffed to an overheating radiator. After being tortured there for three days, he begged to be killed. Instead, DeStefano invited Cappelletti's family to dinner. After they had finished the four-course meal, Cappelletti was brought out, naked and badly burnt, and thrown at the feet of his mother. DeStefano then urinated on him. In some versions of the story, members of Cappelletti's family were forced to urinate on him.

In November 1963, DeStefano paid a visit to the offices of real-estate agent and loan-shark Leo Foreman. There was an argument and Foreman threw him out. On the pretext of making peace, DeStefano lured Foreman to the Cicero home of his brother Mario, who softened him up with a hammer, assisted by Spilotro and Crimaldi. DeStefano then stabbed him 20 times with an ice-pick.

When Foreman pleaded for his life, DeStefano shot him repeatedly in the buttocks, then finished him off with a butcher's knife. Even after Foreman was dead, they continued cutting lumps of flesh from his body.

Crazy courtroom behaviour

In 1972, Crimaldi turned state's evidence and Sam and Mario DeStefano and Spilotro were indicted for Foreman's murder. DeStefano was already said to be crazy, and his courtroom antics became increasingly bizarre. He turned up in his pyjamas, in a wheelchair, and addressed the court through a megaphone. Turning the trial into a circus put it on the front page. This robbed the other defendants of their chance to influence the jury with bribes or by coercion. And it meant Mad Sam had to go.

Just 30 minutes before Spilotro and Mario turned up at DeStefano's house, his wife and bodyguard said they had to go out. DeStefano was gunned down in his garage.

As Spilotro walked free after the Foreman trial, FBI agent Bill Roemer said quietly: 'You're still a little *pissant*. We'll get you yet.'

Spilotro smiled and said: 'F*** you.'

In 1964, 'Mad' Sam DeStefano (centre) leaves court in a characteristically attention-grabbing manner after being sentenced to jail for illegal voting.

GASPIPE

Name: *Anthony Casso*

Aka: *Gaspipe*

Born: *21 May 1940, Brooklyn, New York*

Gang affiliation: *Lucchese*

Convictions: *murder, racketeering, drug trafficking, bank robbery, hijacking*

Anthony 'Gaspipe' Casso is the highest-ranking member of the American Mafia to turn state's evidence. Once the head of the Lucchese family, he says that La Cosa Nostra is 'not an honored society of men anymore, it is a society of self-servicing scumbags that would give up their mother to turn a buck.' But still he hates himself for betraying it.

GROWING UP WITH THE MOB

Casso's grandparents were from Naples and his father was connected. Thanks to his childhood friend Salvatore 'Sally' Callinbrano – later Anthony's godfather and a *capo* in the Genovese family – the family did not go

hungry during the Depression. Callinbrano made sure that Michael Casso had regular work as a longshoreman in the Brooklyn docks and access to the pilfering that went on. A tough guy, Casso Sr. always carried an eight-inch length of lead gas pipe that he used as a weapon. As a result, he was give the nickname 'Gaspipe', which his son inherited.

One of the younger Casso's earliest memories was visiting Callinbrano's club on Flatbush Avenue with his father, where everyone treated the well-dressed *capo* with respect. With the death of Albert Anastasia in 1957, Casso Sr. took over the International Longshoremen's Association Local 1814. When Anthony graduated from the Francis Xavier Catholic Elementary School, Callinbrano gave him a $50 bill. Later he gave him a gold, diamond and sapphire pinkie ring – an essential piece of jewellery for a made man.

On Sundays in summer, the family would go for picnics to Allendale Lake in New Jersey with the families of Joe Profaci, Vito Genovese and Albert Anastasia. There would be target practice with .22 rifles. Casso liked firearms and was a good shot.

In south Brooklyn, Casso was surrounded by the Mafia ethos. Disputes would be settled with the gun or the ice-pick and dead bodies turned up regularly, dumped in Flatbush or in the bays and estuaries around the coast.

In 1954, Casso saw the murder of Joe Monosco on 4th Avenue, followed by Donald Marino's murder on the corner of 5th Avenue and Sackett Street. The next year he witnessed the murder of Frank 'Shoes' De Marco in Costello's Bar. Murder was a way of life in Brooklyn.

BUYING SILENCE

Casso's father took him hunting at the farm of Mafioso Charlie LaRocca in upstate New York. The slaughter of wild animals, Casso later saw, was part of his training for organized crime. He joined a gang named the South Brooklyn Boys and became a notorious street fighter. As a result of one of these fights, Casso was arrested for the first time.

When Casso dropped out of school, Callinbrano supplied him with a forged birth certificate so that he

New York City longshoremen prepare to strike in December 1962. Up until the 1990s, International Longshoremen's Association Local 1814 was a bastion of Mafia power on the Brooklyn waterfront.

Vincent Gigante

a .32 pistol and shot the man in broad daylight. The incident was witnessed by the uncle of Carmine and Allie Persico, Ralph Salerno. While Casso hid out in New Jersey, his father tried to pay off the police, but did not have the $50,000 they demanded. Vincent 'the Chin' Gigante, then a *capo* in the Genovese crime family, offered to pay, but Casso did not want to join the Genovese. Meanwhile, the junkie, who had been badly wounded, was looking for Casso, saying he would kill him. Casso returned to Brooklyn to confront him. But the junkie was also connected. His uncle was a *capo* in the Genovese family and wanted no trouble. Money changed hands. Casso was arrested, but the victim did not identify him and he was acquitted.

COPS ON THE PAYROLL

Casso then went into the hijacking business, arranging for drivers to give up their loads for $10,000, rather than at gunpoint. He also bribed guards so that he could steal from the piers. Soon he was so busy he brought others – including Frankie DeCicco – into the operation.

Casso married and moved into a garden apartment in Bensonhurst and bought his parents a retirement home in the Catskills. By this point he was robbing banks by tunnelling into basement vaults. He carried out a hit for Lucchese made man Christopher Furnari in front of other made men. Then he and DeCicco gunned down a man in the street who had robbed them. Gradually, he built his own crew.

With Vic Amuso, he began importing marijuana from South America. He was soon a wealthy man. But in 1972, on the word of an informant, Casso was arrested. Through Greg Scarpa, he found out who the informant was and bought him off. This made him realize he needed information from the other side. He managed to put two crooked police officers, Louis Eppolito and Stephen Caracappa, on the payroll, along with others including an FBI agent.

could join the longshoremen's union; he also found him a $250-a-week 'no-show job' on the docks.

Through Callinbrano, Casso met Lucchese *capo* 'Christie Tick' Furnari and Paul Castellano, who got him another, more lucrative 'no-show job'. He also collected bookmaking money and loan-sharking receipts, sometimes heavy-handedly.

In 1961, Casso saw a junkie hassling a girl. He intervened and an argument ensued. Casso pulled out

SETTLING SCORES

In 1974, after a long hiatus, the Gambino family books were open again. But Casso became a made man in the Lucchese family instead, and was a member of Vincent 'Vinnie Beans' Foceri's *borgata* (branch of the family), which had its headquarters on 116th Street in Manhattan and 14th Avenue in Brooklyn.

Selling marijuana and cocaine, Casso dealt with Roy DeMeo and Sammy 'the Bull' Gravano. He also took on private work. When the daughter of a friend was raped, he waited until the rapist was out on bail, abducted him, mutilated his genitals, then killed him. And when his wife's 16-year-old nephew was killed by a member of the Colombo family, Casso demanded, and succeeded in getting, his killer's death.

When Furnari became *consigliere* of the Lucchese family, he wanted Casso to become a *capo* and take over his crew. But Casso preferred to be the one soldier a *consigliere* was allowed and recommended Amuso for the post of *capo*. Casso was running a lucrative bootleg gasoline scam with Ukrainian mob boss Marat Balagula in Brighton Beach. When the Russian gangster Vladimir Reznikov tried to muscle in, Casso set him up to be hit by DeMeo's crew.

'After that, Marat didn't have any problems with other Russians,' said Casso.

When Castellano decided that DeMeo had to go, John Gotti and Frankie DeCicco gave the contract to Casso. He, in turn, approached the Testa brothers and Anthony Senter, who did the job.

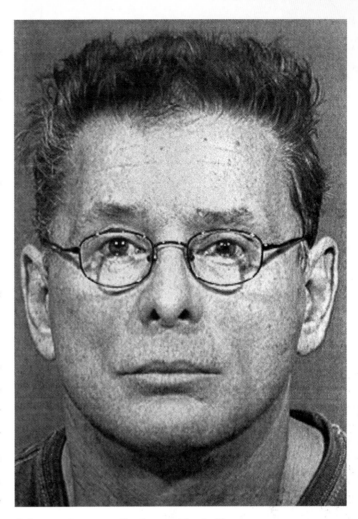

Salvatore Gravano, alias Sammy 'the Bull'

CHILLY HIDING PLACE

The so-called Commission Case followed in 1985, when 11 top Mafiosi, including the heads of the five families, went on trial for racketeering. John Gotti decided that it was time to make his move by hitting Castellano and becoming boss. Casso was against the coup and tried to talk DeCicco out of it, but Gotti had promised to make him underboss.

For killing their boss without permission, Gotti and DeCicco were sentenced to death by the Commission. Casso and Amuso were given the contract and they were told to use a bomb. They learned that Gotti and DeCicco were going to visit a social club in Bensonhurst. When DeCicco's car arrived, Herbie 'Blue Eyes' Pate slipped a bag containing C-4 plastic explosive under it. It was detonated by remote control. DeCicco was killed instantly. Another man with him was badly injured, but Gotti had cancelled at the last moment. They did not get a second chance because Gotti courted publicity and was almost always surrounded by the press. Meanwhile Gotti gave a contract on Casso to a hit team led by James Hydell. Gaspipe was shot at outside the Golden Ox restaurant and sought refuge – from the assassins and the police – in the restaurant's freezer. Hydell paid with his life.

RUNNING THE FAMILY ON THE RUN

The boss of the Lucchese family Tony 'Ducks' Corallo realized that the Commission Case was going to put the leadership of the family away for the rest of their lives. Because Casso was the family's biggest money-maker, Corallo suggested that he should be the new boss. But Casso refused and the leadership passed to Amuso, with Casso as *consigliere* and, later, underboss.

The Mafia had moved in on a $150 million deal from the New York Housing Authority to install replacement windows. In the resulting racketeering investigation, Amuso and Casso were indicted. Tipped off by a mole in the FBI, they went on the run, leaving

> ## *DeCicco was killed instantly . . . another man with him was badly injured*

'Little Al' D'Arco as acting boss.

Even though he was a fugitive, Casso still ordered hits. When 'Fat Pete' Chiodo decided to plead guilty, Casso and Amuso were in danger of being implicated. The two men ordered D'Arco to kill Chiodo. When he failed, Amuso ordered, for the first time in Mafia history, a hit on D'Arco's wife, but she and her children were taken into the Witness Protection Program.

Amuso was captured in a shopping mall in Scranton, Pennsylvania. This left Casso in charge of the Lucchese family. D'Arco realized that he was in danger now and turned himself in to the FBI. Casso continued to run the Lucchese family from the back of a van, but made the mistake of buying new mobile phones that were just being introduced. He was arrested in the shower in his girlfriend's home in Mount Olive, New Jersey.

An attempt to bribe his way out of jail was foiled at the last moment. Casso also planned an ambush on the van that brought him back from court, as well as a hit on the judge. When these ploys failed, he offered to turn state's evidence and pleaded guilty to 72 counts of racketeering, including 15 murders – though it was thought he was responsible for at least 44.

He was sent to a special prison unit for co-operating witnesses, but he would not behave. He got into fights with other prisoners and bribed the guards for favours. The prosecutors decided that he was too unreliable to take the stand against Vincent 'the Chin' Gigante and relied instead on the testimony of D'Arco and Gravano. Casso then wrote a letter claiming they were lying. Clearly, he was not a co-operative witness and he was dropped from the programme. Returned to a regular prison, he was kept in solitary confinement for his own protection. Having broken the terms of his plea bargain, he was sentenced to 13 terms of life imprisonment, plus 455 years.

An FBI surveillance photo of Casso (right) with Amuso.

Louis Eppolito and Stephen Caracappa

When Casso agreed to co-operate with the government in 1994, he gave the authorities the names of two rogue police officers, Louis Eppolito and Stephen Caracappa. These men had not only been informants but had also carried out hits for the mob. They had been on the payroll of the Lucchese family between 1985 and 1993, earning $4,000 a month.

Casso gave the men $65,000 to murder Gambino *capo* Eddie Lino in 1990. The two officers pulled him over on a road leading to the Belt Parkway, Brooklyn and shot him dead. They also set up Bruno Facciolo, a Lucchese soldier who fell out of favour with Casso by failing to visit him when he was recuperating from James Hydell's attempt on his life. Eppolito and Caracappa said they thought Facciolo was working for the FBI. Facciolo was found in the boot of a car with a canary stuffed in his mouth – the mob's traditional warning to informers.

Eppolito and Caracappa cruised Brooklyn and Staten Island looking for James Hydell. They found him in a laundromat, flashed their badges, and told him he was under arrest. Then they put him in the back of an unmarked police car, drove to a back street garage and transferred him to the boot.

Casso was waiting in the Toys 'R' Us car park in Mill Basin. He then took Hydell to a safe house where he beat him up and dragged him into the basement. Casso demanded to know who had ordered the hit. Hydell named Angelo Ruggiero, a Gambino *capo* nicknamed 'Quack Quack' for his uncanny ability to duck indictments.

Gaspipe sent for Gotti and Gravano to see what they had to say about it. They refused to come, but two days later two Gambino *capos*, 'Joe Butch' Corrao and 'Good Looking' Jack Giordano, arrived. They were genuinely shocked at the sight of Hydell. Casso listened to what they had to say, then pulled out a 9 mm Beretta and shot Hydell 15 times before finally killing him.

The Gambino *capos* said they would report what they had seen to Gotti. Casso said that he wanted Ruggiero's head on a plate. He didn't get it. Gotti had bigger things to worry about and Ruggiero died of cancer in 1989.

Eppolito and Caracappa were found guilty of eight counts of murder and conspiracy to murder, along with the obstruction of justice, narcotics trafficking, illegal gambling and labour racketeering. Eppolito was the son of a mobster, a fact he failed to mention when he applied to join the New York Police Department. His uncle and cousin had been murdered by Roy DeMeo and Anthony Gaggi. He was sentenced to life plus 100 years. Caracappa got life plus 80 years. Each was fined more than $4 million. The two continued to protest their innocence.

Stephen Caracappa and Louis Eppolito are transferred to a bus after being flown from Las Vegas to an undisclosed location for prosecution in New York State in 2005.

'NDRANGHETA WARS

Name: *Domenico Condello*

Aka: *Micu 'u pacciù (Crazy Micu)*

Born: *4 November 1956, Reggio Calabria*

Gang affiliation: *'Ndrangheta*

Convictions: *murder, robbery, drugs trafficking, arms trafficking, criminal association*

When he was arrested on 10 October 2012, Domenico Condello topped Italy's 'most wanted' list. He had been on the run for 20 years, yet was found on the outskirts of Calabria's largest city, Reggio Calabria. The day before he was arrested, the city council there was dissolved because of its ties to the 'Ndrangheta, the crime organization that runs the 'toe' of Italy.

Formed in the late 19th century, the 'Ndrangheta considers itself an 'honoured society' like the Camorra in Naples and the Mafia in Sicily. Like them, it is organized around blood ties and observes *omertà* or a code of silence. In the inverted world of organized crime, the name 'Ndrangheta comes from the ancient Greek word for heroism or manly virtue.

THE BUSINESS OF KIDNAPPING

While the 'Ndrangheta confined its activities to rural Calabria, no one took much notice of it, but then it went into the business of kidnapping. Between 1970 and 1991, there were 576 kidnappings in Italy. More than 200 of them were carried out by the 'Ndrangheta. In the province of Reggio Calabria, there is a town named Bovalino. One of its districts is called 'Paul Getty'. This is because, in 1973, John Paul Getty III, the 17-year-old grandson of the oil tycoon Jean Paul Getty, was kidnapped by the 'Ndrangheta. He was held for five months. The family only paid up after the teenager's ear was mailed to them. A month after he was found alive, the members of the

Reggio Calabria, showing its proximity to Sicily across the Strait of Messina

kidnap gang, including a number of 'Ndrangheta bosses, were arrested. Two kidnappers went to jail, but the 'Ndrangheta bosses walked free.

'NDRANGHETA WARS

Until the first war, the 'Ndrangheta was dominated by three regional bosses – Antonio Macrì, Domenico Tripodo and Girolamo Piromalli. The head of the Condello clan – or *'ndrina*, which means 'one who will not bend' – was Pasquale 'Il Supremo' Condello. He is thought to have been one of the squad who killed Antonio Macrì,

the boss of Siderno, who tried to stamp out kidnapping and drug trafficking in 1975. This started a war that consumed at least 300 lives. One of the casualties was Domenico Tripodo, boss of Reggio Calabria. Opposed by his underbosses, the three De Stefano brothers, Tripodo made a pre-emptive strike, killing Giovanni De Stefano before himself being stabbed to death in jail.

Pasquale Condello then allied himself with the De Stefanos. Paolo De Stefano was the best man at his wedding and Pasquale's cousins Domenico and Paolo Condello became the De Stefanos' underbosses. But then their sister Giuseppina married Antonio Imerti, the leader of the 'ndrina in Villa San Giovanni, which faces the Strait of Messina. There were plans to build a bridge across the Strait of Messina to Sicily. As the De Stefanos controlled much of the construction in the province, Paolo feared that this new alliance between the Condellos and the Imerti clan might rob him of some lucrative contracts.

A marriage between Paolo's younger brother Orazio De Stefano and Antonietta Benestare, niece of Giovanni Tegano, head of the 'ndrina of the Archi district, sealed an alliance between the De Stefanos and the Tegano clan. Paolo De Stefano then gave orders that Imerti was to be killed. A bomb attack killed three of his bodyguards, but failed to kill Imerti himself. Two days later, Paolo De Stefano was killed. Domenico and Paolo Condello were arrested for the murder.

Meanwhile the Second 'Ndrangheta War broke out with the Condello, Imerti, Serraino and Rosmini clans on one side, and the De Stefano, Tegano, Libri and Latella clans on the other. Over the next six years, more than 500 people were killed in the fighting.

KEEPING THE PEACE

A peace was eventually brokered by 'Ndrangheta bosses from Canada, including Antonio Imerti's cousin Joe from Ottawa and members of the Zito clan from Toronto, along with a delegation from the Cosa Nostra. To keep the peace, a board of control similar to the Sicilian Commission, named La Provincia, was set up.

In 2007, in Duisburg, Germany, six Italian men were shot dead in an execution-style killing believed to be the work of feuding 'Ndrangheta clans in Calabria.

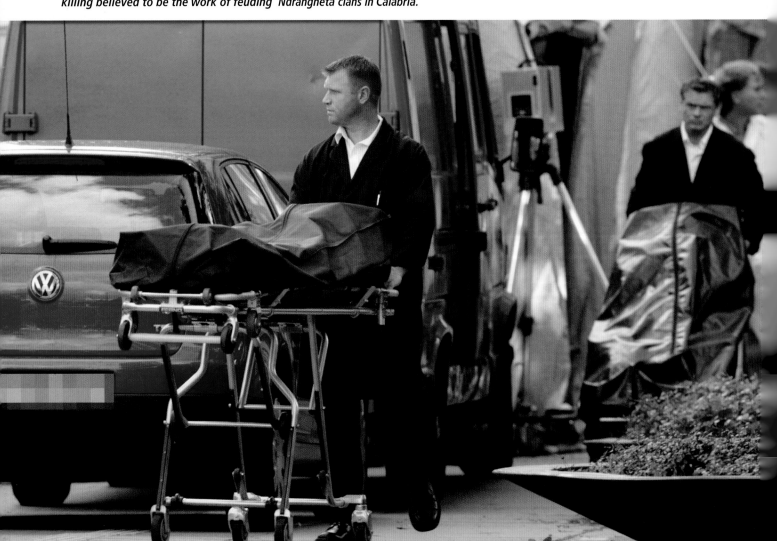

The arrest of Pasquale Condello, one of Italy's most wanted men, on 18 February 2008

Domenico Condello was sentenced to life, but he was released in 1990 because the statute of limitation ran out before his appeal was heard. Meanwhile Pasquale Condello had jumped $100,000 bail after being let out of prison under Italy's leniency rules. Nine arrest warrants were issued for him. While on the run, Pasquale was sentenced *in absentia* to four life terms, plus another 22 years for murder, Mafia association, extortion, money laundering and drug-related offences. He was also accused of ordering one of his hitmen to kill Ludovico Ligato, a former head of the Italian State Railways in 1989.

In 1990 the fugitive Pasquale became a member of La Provincia. Meanwhile Domenico further secured the peace by having two children with Margherita Tegano, though he and his partner did not marry. This left her open to arrest when he went on the run in 1993 and found himself sentenced to life *in absentia*.

COKE MONOPOLY

After the end of the Second 'Ndrangheta War, the Calabrian clans began importing cocaine from Colombia into the container port at Gioia Tauro. By 2006, they were thought to hold a virtual monopoly on cocaine trafficking in Europe, with an annual turnover of some $50 billion.

In February 2008, 100 policemen surrounded the apartment of Pasquale Condello's 30-year-old son-in-law on the outskirts of Reggio Calabria. A crack five-man team from the *carabinieri* burst in. They found Pasquale

On 11 October 2012 Domenico Condello exits the police station in Reggio Calabria, under arrest after almost 20 years on the run.

Condello sitting there, with a bottle of champagne and a bottle of fine French brandy on the table. He put up no resistance and was quickly whisked away to northern Italy for interrogation. Domenico succeeded Pasquale as boss and took his place on the 'most wanted' list.

CUTTING THE TENTACLES

Maintaining close family ties, the 'Ndrangheta remains the most difficult Italian crime organization to crack. Justice authorities in Italy have rated the 'Ndrangheta as the most dangerous existing form of organized crime and believe that the super-secretive organization works with Turkish and Albanian mobs

and, through the latter, with the Russian Mafia.

The tentacles of the 'Ndrangheta reached Milan. Wiretaps and secret recordings of members of the Condello clan revealed that they had business contacts with the brothers Giulio, Giuseppe and Francesco Lampada, who were originally from Reggio Calabria but had left to establish themselves in the north of Italy. As the noose tightened, Margherita Tegano, along with Condello's cousins Caterina and Giuseppa Condello and 15 others, were arrested for obstructing Condello's capture.

Then on 10 October 2012, Domenico Condello himself was finally brought to book.

Sacra Corona Unita

Along with the Mafia of Sicily, the Camorra of Naples and the 'Ndrangheta of Calabria, there is another crime organization in southern Italy – the Sacra Corona Unita (United Sacred Crown) of Puglia, the 'heel' of the Italian peninsula.

The so-called 'fourth Mafia' was set up in the 1970s when Camorrista Raffaele Cutolo decided to expand his operations into Puglia to make use of the Adriatic ports. He then began collaborating with local gangs. By the end of the decade he had formed the Nuova Grande Camorra Pugliese.

However, back in Naples, Cutolo's Nuova Camorra Organizzata was losing ground to the rival Nuova Famiglia. It lost hundreds of soldiers in the 1980–83 Camorra War and in 1983 Cutolo and 1,000 members of the NCO were rounded up by the police.

With Cutolo out of the way, the mobsters in Puglia were formed into the Sacra Corona Unita by Umberto Bellocco of the 'Ndrangheta, who wanted to oppose Camorra influence in Puglia. They offered local crooks a better deal as they did not demand a share of their illicit profits. When Bellocco was also jailed, Giuseppe Rogoli took over the SCU as an autonomous organization, even though he was in Bari prison at the time.

Using the Mafia as his model, Rogoli moved in on wine and olive oil interests. The SCU then committed a series of frauds, swindles and extortions before engaging in cigarette smuggling and arms and drug trafficking. Soon the SCU developed alliances with its counterparts in Albania, Romania and Russia and received pay-offs from other crime outfits for landing rights on the southeast coast.

The SCU is composed of three *società* or groupings: the Società Minore, the Società Maggiore and the Società Segreta – Minor, Major and Secret. Candidates must have no police connections. After a period of probation, they are required to swear the oath: 'I swear on the point of this fist, to be faithful to this formal societal body, to reject father, mother, brothers and sisters, up to the seventh generation; I swear to divide hundredth per hundredth and thousandth per thousandth until the last droplet of blood, with one foot in the grave and the other chained in order to give a strong embrace to prison.'

Recruits to the Società Minore must renounce all other affiliations and owe their only allegiance to the SCU. The *picciotto* or apprentice is then formally inducted into the organization as a *manovalanza* or worker.

The Società Maggiore has two ranks: Lo Sgarro and La Santa. To become a *Sgarro*, you must have committed at least three killings ordered by the SCU. The *Sgarro* are identified by a rose tattoo and can only leave the organization on pain of death. A *Sgarro* occupies a designated territory and can form a *filiale*, a branch or clan of *picciotti*, who report to him.

Sgarri who do well graduate to become *Sante* in a rite performed at midnight. During this ceremony they are given a cyanide pill, a rifle or a pistol, a lemon, a wad of cotton wool, a needle, three white silk handkerchiefs and the so-called *spartenza*, which means 'a division of spoils'. The cyanide allows the *Santa* to choose death rather than collaborate with the authorities and the firearm is for the same purpose, to be used on himself if he fails to live up to the expectations of the SCU. The lemon is to tend the wounds of comrades; the cotton wool represents Mont Blanc – or Monte Bianco – which is considered sacred; the needle is to puncture the index finger of the right hand; the lemon juice is mixed with the blood as another sign of fidelity; the handkerchiefs represent purity of spirit; and the *spartenza* usually consists of a gift of cigarettes.

Within the Società Segreta, there is the General Council, which makes the decisions. Those who reach those heights have to swear: 'I would rather rip out my heart and hand it to my *padrino*, have it sliced and distributed to the General Council than betray my sacred brotherhood. I swear, moreover, solemnly, in both good and bad, in calm and tempest, my *padrino* is inviolable, my brother of blood, and not even a universal flood can put an end to this union, sealed with our blood.'

The SCU consists of some 50 clans with around 2,000 members. Vendettas are particularly brutal. According to one report: 'Often the victim's body is brutally tortured in a procedure of death and revenge. Gouged eyes, severed tongues or genitals, each method of killing corresponds to a sort of Dantesque passage that reveals the "sin" that irreparably stained the sinner.'

To date, the Sacra Corona Unita has made little headway in North America.

DIABOLIK

Name: *Matteo Messina Denaro*

Aka: *Diabolik, Alessio*

Born: *26 April 1962, Castelvetrano, Trapani, Sicily*

Family affiliation: *Denaro*

Charges: *murder, terrorism, theft, extortion, loan-sharking, money-laundering, fraud, criminal association*

Matteo Messina Denaro is a new type of Mafia don, not least because he has slipped the old Mafia's moral straitjacket and has emerged as a ladies' man – in defiance of the old Sicilian proverb that giving orders is better than sex.

LEGEND IN HIS OWN TIME

Some Mafiosi worship Messina Denaro as a saint. Others see him as James Bond – he is said to have an Alfa Romeo 164 armed with machine guns that can be activated at the push of a button. He boasts that he has filled a cemetery all by himself. It is said he is the guardian of Totò Riina's treasure which includes not only a fabulous collection of jewellery, but also the Mafia archive. This is purportedly held in a secret vault under a jeweller's shop in Castelvetrano, which can only be entered using an elevator built into the strongroom. However, his police files give his profession as 'farmer'.

His father, Francesco Messina Denaro, aka Don Ciccio, was a member of the Cupola, or Mafia Commission, and an ally of the Corleone faction led by Totò Riina and Bernardo Provenzano. He and his two sons, Matteo and Salvatore, were on the payroll of one of the richest families in Trapani. Among its number is Senator Antonio D'Ali, who claimed he had no idea that the Messina Denaros were involved in the Mafia. Francesco and Matteo were employed as estate managers – a traditional job for Mafiosi – while Salvatore was a clerk in the senator's family bank.

Matteo's brother-in-law, Giuseppe Guttadauro, was also a Mafia boss, even though he practised as a doctor.

He received patients in his surgery each evening between 5 and 7 pm, after it had been open to the *picciotti* who had been collecting protection money.

MYOPIC KILLER

Taught to shoot at 14, Matteo killed for the first time at 18. His father found him a job as an armed guard to the D'Ali family. During the Mafia wars, he worked for Totò Riina. When Riina ordered the execution of Vincenzo Milazzo, Denaro killed him and strangled his pregnant girlfriend for good measure.

He served as Riina's chief intelligence officer and spied on anti-Mafia judge Giovanni Falcone and former justice minister Claudio Martelli, while both were living in Rome in the early 1990s. He also plotted the attack on the TV host Maurizio Costanzo.

In 1993, on Riina's orders, Denaro carried out car bomb attacks on the Uffizi Gallery in Florence and the Basilica of St John Lateran in Rome, which killed ten people and injured 93 others. Law enforcement officials also hold Denaro directly responsible for the murder of another six people, though he claimed to have killed more than 50.

After the bombing campaign, he went underground, using the pseudonym 'Alessio' in his clandestine correspondence with Bernardo Provenzano. It is thought that he attended a clinic in Barcelona, Spain, to treat his myopia.

However, while being on the list of the world's ten most wanted fugitives, he remained curiously well known. Addicted to video games, he rejoices in the soubriquet of 'Diabolik', after an Italian comic strip character.

THE PLAYBOY DON

According to the press, Messina Denaro is a notorious womanizer who revels in the high life, with an extensive

Trapani on the west coast of Sicily – Diabolik's birthplace

collection of Porsches, designer watches and sharp suits. A detective at Trapani police headquarters said: 'Messina Denaro is generous, he's an effortless conversationalist and he can judge the *perlage* of a fine champagne.'

He can afford to. He is worth an estimated $3.7 billion.

Time magazine called him the 'playboy don'.

Giacomo Di Girolamo, author of *The Invisible*, a book on the mobster, says: 'Denaro is a modern Mafia boss, the opposite of the traditional image of *The Godfather*. He has numerous lovers and a child out of wedlock. He knows which businesses to get involved in – and this is primarily drugs.'

His daughter lives with her grandmother in Castelvetrano, along with her mother – who dare not look another man in the eye because she needs to preserve the

In 1993, Denaro carried out a car-bomb attack on the Uffizi Gallery in Florence.

with the South American drug cartels and masterminds the importation of heroin and cocaine into Europe. As well as loan-sharking and extortion, Denaro has moved the Mafia into a new area of moneymaking – renewable energy.

Land is bought at a fraction of its true value and sold at a huge profit to developers who want to build solar and wind farms. Then the European Union hands out millions of euros for their construction. Investments are used to launder Mafia money.

The scale of the operation was revealed when police seized assets worth $1.8 billion from Sicilian businessman Vito Nicastri, who is nicknamed the 'God of the Wind' and is said to be a frontman for Denaro. They included more than 40 companies, nearly 100 properties, seven sports cars and luxury yachts. It was said to be the 'biggest ever seizure of assets linked to Denaro'.

Sicily is dotted with these giant windmills and solar panels, but they have never been connected to the grid. All are sitting there, laundering mob money.

All the police have to go on are snapshots of Denaro taken 20 years ago. In a bid to track him down they have used a special computer programme to age his image, but they admit that this may be of very little use as he is believed to have undergone extensive plastic surgery.

reputation of her errant lover and her own life.

In 2001 the Italian news magazine *L'Espresso* put him on their cover with the caption: 'He is the new boss of the Mafia.' The magazine also reported that Denaro had killed a Sicilian hotel owner who had accused him of bedding young girls.

GREEN ENERGY CHAMPION

But it was only with the arrest of Provenzano in 2006 that Denaro became 'don of dons'. He did so only then as the result of a vicious Mafia war. According to Di Girolamo: 'Denaro is without doubt a very powerful and ruthless man who will stop at nothing to ensure he has utmost control of his territory.'

The FBI say Denaro is the Mafia's principal connection

FOLK HERO

The other strategy open to them is to strip him of his assets. Building firms, cement companies, houses and shops worth around £455 million have been confiscated, along with supermarkets, which are one of the Mafia's main outlets for money laundering. But the forced closure of many branches has angered locals, who see Denaro as their benefactor. He provides job for them in the supermarkets and distribution centres that the Mafia have built for money laundering.

'The problem is many people in Sicily feel they have been abandoned by the Italian state,' said Di Girolamo, 'and see Denaro as a heavenly provider. He has given them jobs and money where the state has given them nothing so that's why many are attracted to the Mafia.'

Denaro's name has also been linked to a money-laundering account in the Vatican bank. In all, the state has seized $3.8 billion from him since 2009.

Di Girolamo is convinced Denaro has politicians and police officers on his payroll. He says: 'How else do you explain the fact that Denaro has been on the run for almost 20 years? He has a network of allies and is always on the move – I doubt he is abroad. If he left his home territory then it would be a sign of weakness and he could lose his grip. I am certain that senior figures within Italian politics and the police are doing their utmost to keep him in hiding.'

Denaro was in the news again in May 2013, when a trial opened in Palermo. It involved senior politicians, who were accused of entering into secret talks with the Cosa Nostra during Denaro's bombing campaign in the 1990s.

The elusive Denaro remains a folk hero. People reminisce about giving him a lift or having smoked with him and he is said to have the same appeal as the charismatic Mexican revolutionary Emiliano Zapata. One local mobster, caught on a wiretap planning to abandon his wife and daughter to join his idol on the run, said: 'Better one day as a lion than a hundred as a sheep.'

A composite 'age progression' identikit image of Denaro, who has been on the run since 1993.

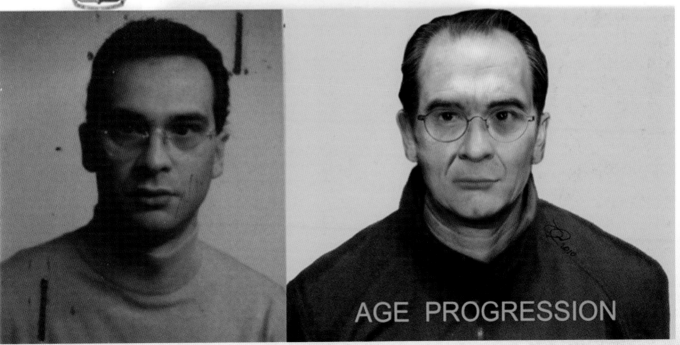

Big Business

According to the Italian trade association Confesercenti, the Mafia is Italy's richest company with a turnover of more than $172 billion in 2012. It makes a profit of $124 billion, which is equivalent to 7 per cent of the country's gross domestic product.

Confesercenti says that the Mafia is also the biggest bank in Italy with liquid assets of $80 billion. Thanks to extortion and intimidation, millions are handed over in protection money by shopkeepers, restaurant owners, cinemas, construction firms and thousands of other businesses. However, its loan-sharking and extortion practices have led to the closure of more than 190,000 businesses in the previous three years.

The 'Ndrangheta alone turned over $56 billion in 2008 from cocaine, gun-running, human trafficking and extortion rackets. The proceeds are laundered through 'legitimate' businesses such as bars, hotels, pizzerias and factories across Europe,

Archbishop Marcinkus, head of the Vatican bank from 1971-89, was implicated in financial scandals.

often contracting out operations through alliances with foreign criminal organizations, particularly from China.

According to *pentito* Giuseppe Di Bella, the breakthrough came in 1992, when 'Ndrangheta bosses met their Chinese counterparts in a basement storeroom near Milan to discuss sharing out markets in textiles, clothing, restaurants and other outlets.

'It wasn't just a local agreement; it was a big deal; they were carving up the whole of Italy,' he said.

Drug dealing was outsourced to Africans; Albanians were first given a remit for prostitution and later arms; the Slavs specialized in trafficking women and were used as hitmen 'when accounts needed settling'.

The recession plays into Mafia hands too, 'their supermarket trolley piled high with bankrupt businesses, answerable to no one', said Di Bella. Bound tightly by almost impenetrable family ties, the 'Ndrangheta has corrupted its way into the political world, organs of government, trade unions, courts and the police. Local elections are rigged and politicians reward their sponsors, often with construction contracts.

The 'Ndrangheta is believed to dominate the earth-moving equipment sector in northern Italy and the billion-dollar cake of Expo 2015 – the universal exposition to be hosted by Milan – has already been sliced up.

Di Bella gives a chilling picture of the 'Ndrangheta's business methods. A wealthy accountant, who had already been beaten up by his abductors, had a rope tied around his ankles and was lowered slowly from a railway bridge into the moonlit river Adda, some 60 feet below.

'We put his head underwater for about a minute and then pulled him up to let him breathe for another three minutes,' said Di Bella. 'He started screaming, louder and louder. We repeated the process about ten times, until he gave in. By then his voice was so shrill it sounded like a woman's. He promised to do anything we asked him to do. Of course, we wanted his buildings.'

This did not happen in Calabria, or in the Mafia heartland of Sicily or southern Italy, but near the picturesque lakeside town of Lecco, close to the Swiss border.